easy to make!
Hot & Spicy

Good Housekeeping

easy to make!
Hot & Spicy

COLLINS & BROWN

First published in Great Britain in 2009
by Collins & Brown
10 Southcombe Street
London W14 0RA

An imprint of Anova Books Company Ltd

The Good Housekeeping website is
www.allaboutyou.com/goodhousekeeping

1 2 3 4 5 6 7 8 9

ISBN 978-1-84340-501-6

A catalogue record for this book is available from the British
Library.

Reproduction by Dot Gradations Ltd
Printed and bound by Times Offset, Malaysia

This book can be ordered direct from the publisher. Contact the
marketing department, but try your bookshop first.

www.anovabooks.com

NOTES

- Both metric and imperial measures are given for the recipes. Follow either set of measures, not a mixture of both, as they are not interchangeable.
- All spoon measures are level.
  1 tsp = 5ml spoon; 1 tbsp = 15ml spoon.
- Ovens and grills must be preheated to the specified temperature.
- Use sea salt and freshly ground black pepper unless otherwise suggested.
- Fresh herbs should be used unless dried herbs are specified in a recipe.
- Medium eggs should be used except where otherwise specified. Free-range eggs are recommended.
- Note that certain recipes, including mayonnaise, lemon curd and some cold desserts, contain raw or lightly cooked eggs. The young, elderly, pregnant women and anyone with an immune-deficiency disease should avoid these, because of the slight risk of salmonella.
- Calorie, fat and carbohydrate counts per serving are provided for the recipes.
- If you are following a gluten- or dairy-free diet, check the labels on all pre-packaged food goods.
- Recipe serving suggestions do not take gluten- or dairy-free diets into account.

Picture Credits

Photographers: Neil Barclay (pages 37, 57, 77); Martin Brigdale
(pages 38, 69, 75, 79, 80, 82, 85, 105, 108); Nicki Dowey (pages
32, 33, 34, 39, 40, 42, 43, 44, 45, 47, 53, 54, 56, 59, 61, 64, 68,
71, 72, 84, 86, 91, 93, 94, 97, 99, 102, 103, 104, 107, 113, 117,
119, 121, 123, 125); Will Heap (page 109); Craig Robertson
(Basics photography plus pages 36, 50, 51, 58, 62, 63, 76,
78, 83, 95, 98, 100, 110, 116, 118, 120, 124, 126); Lucinda
Symons (pages 28, 90, 106);

Contents

Foreword

Spices are one of the quickest and easiest ways of adding depth and flavour to lots of dishes. Add a pinch of chilli flakes to the onion when you're making a simple tomato sauce for pasta and you'll be rewarded with a gentle warmth in the finished dish. Next time you're having hummus, stir in a sprinkling of freshly toasted cumin seeds for an earthy middle-eastern bite or add a pinch of ground cloves to pot of red cabbage for a sweet fragrant taste.

This new book in the Good Housekeeping Easy To Make Series, shows you how to use spice in everything – whether it's a light meal or a more substantial supper. There's a wealth of inspiring recipes – salads, rice and vegetable dishes, warming one-pot stews and easy meals when you're pushed for time and need to get something on the table quickly. I have my eye on the curried lamb with lentils and will serve it with a drizzle of natural yogurt and freshly chopped coriander along with rice or naan bread to soak up the zingy sauce, and the Thai crab balls with a homemade sweet chilli sauce will also become firm favourites.

We've also included a handy basics chapter which covers everything from chopping an onion to preparing fresh root ginger, garlic and chillies. All the recipes have been triple tested in the Good Housekeeping kitchens to make sure they work every time for you. Enjoy!

Emma

Emma Marsden
Cookery Editor
Good Housekeeping

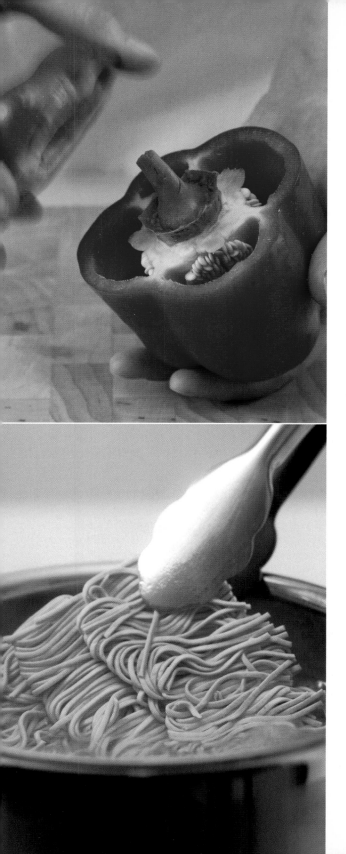

The Basics

Spices and their uses

Most spices are sold dried, either whole or ground. For optimum flavour, buy whole spices and grind them yourself.

Dry-frying spices

Spices are often toasted in a dry heavy-based frying pan to mellow their flavour and lose any raw taste. Spices can be dry-fried individually or as mixtures. Put the hardest ones, such as fenugreek, into the pan first and add softer ones, like coriander and cumin, after a minute or so. Stir constantly until evenly browned. Cool, then grind, or crush in a pestle and mortar and use the toasted spices as required.

Allspice, also called Jamaica pepper, is sold as small dried berries or ready ground. It tastes like a mixture of cloves, cinnamon and nutmeg. Allspice can be used whole in marinades, meat dishes, pickles, chutneys and with poached fish. Ground allspice is added to meat and vegetable dishes, cakes, milk puddings and fruit pies.

Cardamom, available as small green and large black pods containing seeds, has a strong aromatic quality and should be used sparingly. Add cardamom pods whole and remove before serving, or extract the seeds and use these whole or grind them to a powder just before use. Cardamom is a component of most curry powders.

Cayenne pepper is made from small, hot dried red chillies. It is always sold ground and is sweet, pungent and very hot. Use it sparingly. Unlike paprika, cayenne pepper cannot be used for colouring as its flavour is too pronounced.

Chilli, available as powder or flakes as well as fresh, is a fiery hot spice and should be used cautiously. Some brands, often called mild chilli powder or chilli seasoning, are a mixture of chilli and other flavourings, such as cumin, oregano, salt and garlic; these are therefore considerably less fiery than hot chilli powder. Adjust the quantity you use accordingly.

Cinnamon is the dried, rolled bark of a tropical evergreen tree. Available as sticks and in powdered form, it has a sweet, pungent flavour. Cinnamon sticks have a more pronounced flavour than the powder, but they are difficult to grind at home, so buy ready-ground cinnamon for use in sweet, spicy baking. Use cinnamon sticks to flavour meat casseroles, vegetable dishes, chutneys and pickles.

Cloves are the dried flower buds of an evergreen tree. Strong and pungent, they are one of the ingredients of five-spice powder.

Coriander seeds have a mild, sweet, orangey flavour and taste quite different from the fresh green leaves, which are used as a herb. Sold whole or ground, they are an ingredient of most curry powders.

Cumin has a strong, slightly bitter taste, improved by toasting. Sold whole as seeds, or ground, it is an ingredient of curry powders and some chilli powder mixtures.

Curry leaves These shiny leaves have a fresh-tasting flavour akin to curry powder. They are used as a herb in cooking, most often added whole, but sometimes chopped first. The fresh or dried leaves can be used sparingly to flavour soups and stews. Sold fresh in bunches, curry leaves can be frozen in a plastic bag and added to dishes as required.

Fenugreek seeds are yellow-brown and very hard, with a distinctive aroma and slightly harsh, hot flavour. An ingredient of commercial curry powders, fenugreek is also used in chutneys, pickles and sauces.

Furikake seasoning is a Japanese condiment consisting of sesame seeds and chopped dried seaweed. It can be found in major supermarkets and Asian food shops.

Mustard seeds come from three different mustard plants, which produce black, brown and white (or yellow) seeds. The darker seeds are more pungent than the light ones. Most ready-prepared mustards are a combination of the different seeds in varying proportions. The seeds are either left whole (as in wholegrain mustard) or ground, then mixed with liquid such as wine, vinegar or cider. English mustard is sold as a dry yellow powder, or ready-mixed.

Nutmeg, seed of the nutmeg fruit, has a distinctive, nutty flavour. Sold whole or ground, but best bought whole since the flavour of freshly grated nutmeg is far superior.

Paprika is a sweet mild spice made from certain varieties of red pepper; it is always sold ground to a red powder.

It is good for adding colour to pale egg and cheese dishes. Some varieties, particularly Hungarian, are hotter than others. Paprika doesn't keep its flavour well, so buy little and often. Produced from oak-smoked red peppers, **smoked paprika** has an intense flavour and wonderful smoky aroma. Sweet, bittersweet and hot-smoked varieties are available.

Saffron, the most expensive of all spices, is the dried stigma of the saffron crocus flower. It has a wonderful subtle flavour and aroma, and imparts a hint of yellow to foods it is cooked with. Powdered saffron is available, but it is the whole stigmas, called saffron strands or threads, that give the best results. A generous pinch is all that is needed to flavour and colour dishes.

Star anise, the attractive, dried, star-shaped fruit of an evergreen tree native to China, is red-brown in colour with a pungent aniseed flavour. It is strong, so use sparingly, either whole or ground. Ground star anise is used in five-spice powder.

Turmeric is a member of the ginger family, though it is rarely available fresh. The bright orange root is commonly dried, then ground and sold in powdered form. Turmeric powder has an aromatic, slightly bitter flavour and should be used sparingly in curry powder, pickles, relishes and rice dishes. Like saffron, turmeric colours the foods it is cooked with, but it has a much harsher flavour than saffron.

Spice mixes

Curry powder - bought curry powders are readily available, but for optimum flavour make your own.
To make your own curry powder: Put 1 tbsp each cumin and fenugreek seeds, 1/2 tsp mustard seeds, 1 1/2 tsp each poppy seeds, black peppercorns and ground ginger, 4 tbsp coriander seeds, 1/2 tsp hot chilli powder and 2 tbsp ground turmeric into an electric blender or grinder. Grind to a fine powder. Store the curry powder in an airtight container and use within one month.

Five-spice powder - a powerful, pungent ground mixture of star anise, Szechuan pepper, fennel seeds, cloves and cinnamon or cassia. Use sparingly.

Garam masala - sold ready-prepared, this Indian spice mix is aromatic rather than hot.
To make your own garam masala: Grind together 10 green cardamom pods, 1 tbsp black peppercorns and 2 tsp cumin seeds. Store in an airtight container and use within one month.

Tikka masala - sold ready-prepared as a powder or paste, this spice mix is used with creamed coconut and/or yogurt as the basis of a sauce for chicken, meat or fish.

Pastes, sauces and oils

Ready-made pastes and sauces, consisting of ingredients such as spices, fresh chillies, onion, ginger and oil, are widely available, but most are also easily made at home. Knowing which oil to use in your cooking will greatly improve the finished dishes – some oils are general purpose, some should be used only for cooking, while others, because their tastes are intense, work best as a flavouring.

Pastes

Balti paste Balti is a curry named after the flat-bottomed steel pot in which it is cooked and served.
To make your own balti paste: Put 1 tbsp each fennel seeds and ground allspice, 2–3 roughly chopped garlic cloves, a 1cm (1/2in) piece fresh root ginger, peeled and roughly chopped, 50g (2oz) garam masala, 25g (1oz) curry powder and 1 tsp salt into a food processor with 8 tbsp water and blend. Divide the paste into three equal portions, then freeze for up to three months.

Harissa is a spicy paste flavoured with chillies, coriander and caraway and is used as a condiment or ingredient in North African cooking, particularly in Morocco, Tunisia and Algeria.
To make your own harissa: Grill 2 red peppers until softened and charred, cool, then skin, core and seed. Put 4 seeded and roughly chopped red chillies in a food processor with 6 peeled garlic cloves, 1 tbsp ground coriander and 1 tbsp caraway seeds. Process to a rough paste, then add the grilled peppers, 2 tsp salt and 4 tbsp olive oil, and whiz until smooth. Put the harissa into a screwtopped jar, cover with a thin layer of olive oil and store in the refrigerator for up to two weeks.

Korma paste is a mild Indian curry paste.
To make your own korma paste: Put 3 tbsp ground cinnamon, seeds from 36 green cardamom pods, 30 cloves, 18 bay leaves, 1 tbsp fennel seeds and 1 tsp salt into a food processor and blend to a powder. Tip the powder into a bowl and add 4 tbsp water, stirring well to make a paste. Divide into three equal portions, then freeze for up to three months.

Laksa paste is a spicy Asian paste made from several ingredients including ginger, garlic, coriander root, shrimp paste, lemongrass and chillies.

Madras paste is a hot and spicy Indian curry paste.
To make your own madras paste: Put 1 finely chopped small onion, a 2.5cm (1in) piece fresh root ginger, peeled and finely chopped, 2 crushed garlic cloves, juice of 1/2 lemon, 1 tbsp each cumin seeds and coriander seeds, 1 tsp cayenne pepper, 2 tsp each ground turmeric and garam masala and 1 tsp salt into a food processor with 2 tbsp water and blend until smooth. Divide the paste into three equal portions, then freeze for up to three months.

Massaman paste is a Thai curry paste. The ingredients include red chillies, roasted shallots, roasted garlic, galangal, lemongrass, roasted coriander seeds, roasted cumin, roasted cloves, white pepper, salt and shrimp paste. It's available in supermarkets or Asian food stores.

Tamarind is the pulp that surrounds the seeds within the large pods of the Indian tamarind tree. Dark brown, with a fresh, acidic flavour, it is generally sold dried and compressed into blocks. To use, simply break off pieces and reconstitute to make tamarind juice. It's used to add a sour flavour to chutneys, sauces and curries. Ready-made tamarind paste is available in jars from large supermarkets. Lime or lemon juice can be substituted for tamarind if necessary.
To extract tamarind juice: Soak 1 tbsp dried tamarind pulp in 4 tbsp warm water for 20 minutes, then strain the liquid through a sieve, pressing hard to extract as much juice from the pulp as possible.

Tandoori paste is used on foods such as chicken and fish to add flavour and to give it a reddish-orange colour common in tandoor cooking.
To make your own tandoori paste: Put 24 crushed garlic cloves, a 5cm (2in) piece fresh root ginger, peeled and chopped, 3 tbsp each coriander seeds, cumin seeds, ground fenugreek and paprika, 3 seeded and chopped red chillies, 3 tsp English mustard, 2 tbsp tomato purée and 1 tsp salt into a food processor with 8 tbsp water and blend to a paste. Divide the paste into three equal portions, then freeze for up to three months.

Thai green curry paste is a blend of spices such as green chillies, coriander and lemongrass. **Thai red curry paste** contains fresh and dried red chillies and ginger. Once opened, store in a sealed container in the refrigerator.

Wasabi paste is a Japanese condiment, green in colour and extremely hot – a little goes a long way. It is available from some supermarkets, but if you can't get it, use creamed horseradish instead.

Sauces

Soy sauce – made from fermented soya beans and, usually, wheat, this is the most common flavouring in Chinese and South-east Asian cooking. There are light and dark soy sauces; the dark kind is slightly sweeter and tends to darken the food. It will keep indefinitely.

Tabasco – a fiery hot sauce based on red chillies, spirit vinegar and salt, and prepared to a secret recipe. A dash of Tabasco may be used to add a kick to soups, casseroles, sauces, rice dishes and tomato-based drinks.

Tamari – similar to soy sauce, this fermented sauce is made from soya beans and is dark in colour and rich in flavour. Usually wheat-free.

Teriyaki sauce – a Japanese sauce made from soy sauce, mirin (a sweet Japanese cooking wine) and sugar.

Thai fish sauce – a salty condiment with a distinctive, pungent aroma. It is used in many South-east Asian dishes. You can buy it in most large supermarkets and Asian food stores. It will keep indefinitely.

Coconut milk

Canned coconut milk is widely available, but if you can't find it, use blocks of **creamed coconut** or **coconut powder**, following the packet instructions to make the amount of liquid you need.

Which oil to use?

Groundnut (peanut) oil has a mild flavour and is well suited to stir-frying and deep-frying as it has a high smoke point and can therefore be used at high temperatures.
Sesame oil has a distinctive nutty flavour; it is best used in marinades or added as a seasoning to stir-fried dishes just before serving.
Vegetable oil may be pure cold-pressed rapeseed oil, sunflower oil, or a blend of corn, soya bean, rapeseed or other oils. It usually has a bland flavour and is suitable for stir-frying.

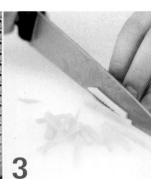

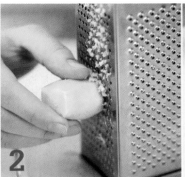

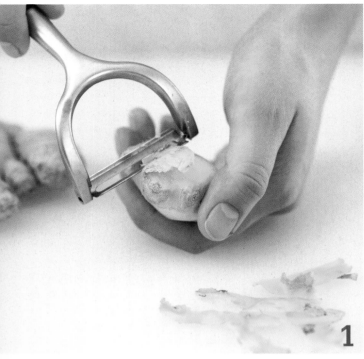

Ginger

1 **Grating** Cut off a piece of the root and peel with a vegetable peeler. Cut off any brown spots.

2 Rest the grater on a board or small plate and grate the ginger. Discard any large fibres adhering to the pulp.

3 **Slicing, shredding and chopping** Cut slices off the ginger and cut off the skin carefully. Cut off any brown spots. Stack the slices and cut into shreds. To chop, stack the shreds and cut across into small pieces.

4 **Pressing** If you just need the ginger juice, peel and cut off any brown spots, then cut into small chunks and use a garlic press held over a small bowl to extract the juice.

Flavourings

Many stir-fry recipes begin by cooking garlic, ginger and spring onions as the basic flavourings. Spicier dishes may include chillies, lemongrass or a prepared spice paste such as Thai curry paste.

Lemongrass

Lemongrass is a popular South-east Asian ingredient, giving an aromatic lemony flavour. It looks rather like a long, slender spring onion, but is fibrous and woody and is usually removed before the dish is served. Alternatively, the inner leaves may be very finely chopped or pounded in a mortar and pestle and used in spice pastes. Dried and powdered lemongrass are also available.

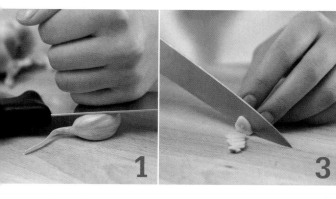

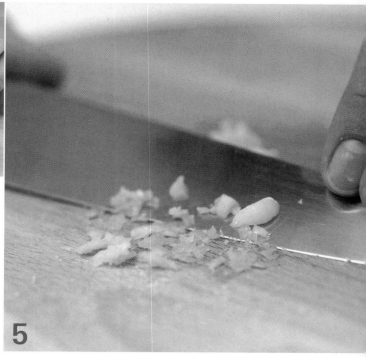

Garlic

1 Put the clove on a chopping board and place the flat side of a large knife on top of it. Press down firmly on the flat of the blade to crush the clove and break the papery skin.

2 Cut off the base of the clove and slip the garlic out of its skin. It should come away easily.

3 **Slicing** Using a rocking motion with the knife tip on the board, slice the garlic as thinly as you need.

4 **Shredding and chopping** Holding the slices together, shred them across the slices. Chop the shreds if you need chopped garlic.

5 **Crushing** After step 2, the whole clove can be put into a garlic press. To crush with a knife: roughly chop the peeled cloves with a pinch of salt. Press down hard with the edge of a large knife tip (with the blade facing away from you), then drag the blade along the garlic while still pressing hard. Continue to do this, dragging the knife tip over the garlic.

Chillies

1 Cut off the cap and slit the chilli open lengthways. Using a spoon, scrape out the seeds and the pith.

2 For diced chilli, cut into thin shreds lengthways, then cut crossways.

Cook's Tip

Wash hands thoroughly after handling chillies – the volatile oils will sting if accidentally rubbed into your eyes.

Washing

1 Trim the roots and part of the stalks from the herbs. Immerse in cold water and shake briskly. Leave in the water for a few minutes.

2 Lift out of the water and put in a colander or sieve, then rinse again under the cold tap. Leave to drain for a few minutes, then dry thoroughly on kitchen paper or teatowels, or use a salad spinner.

Using herbs

Most herbs are the leaf of a flowering plant, and are usually sold with much of the stalk intact. They have to be washed, trimmed and then chopped or torn into pieces suitable for your recipe.

Chopping

1 Trim the herbs by pinching off all but the smallest, most tender stalks. If the herb is one with a woody stalk, such as rosemary or thyme, it may be easier to remove the leaves by rubbing the whole bunch between your hands; the leaves should simply pull off the stems.

2 If you are chopping the leaves, gather them into a compact ball in one hand, keeping your fist around the ball (but being careful not to crush them).

3 Chop with a large knife, using a rocking motion and letting just a little of the ball out of your fingers at a time.

4 When the herbs are roughly chopped, continue chopping until the pieces are in small shreds or flakes.

Perfect herbs

- After washing, don't pour the herbs and their water into the sieve, because dirt in the water might get caught in the leaves.
- If the herb has fleshy stalks, such as parsley or coriander, the stalks can be saved to flavour stock or soup. Tie them in a bundle with string for easy removal.

Preparing vegetables

These frequently used vegetables can be quickly prepared to add flavour to spicy dishes: onions and shallots have a pungent taste that becomes milder when they are cooked, and are often used as a basic flavouring, while tomatoes and peppers add depth and richness to a variety of dishes.

Onions

1 Cut off the tip and base of the onion. Peel away all the layers of papery skin and any discoloured layers underneath.

2 Put the onion root end down on the chopping board, then, using a sharp knife, cut the onion in half from tip to base.

3 **Slicing** Put one half on the board with the cut surface facing down and slice across the onion.

4 **Chopping** Slice the halved onions from the root end to the top at regular intervals. Next, make 2–3 horizontal slices through the onion, then slice vertically across the width.

Shallots

1 Cut off the tip and trim off the ends of the root. Peel off the skin and any discoloured layers underneath.

2 Holding the shallot with the root end down, use a small, sharp knife to make deep parallel slices almost down to the base while keeping the slices attached to it.

3 **Slicing** Turn the shallot on its side and cut off slices from the base.

4 **Dicing** Make deep parallel slices at right angles to the first slices. Turn the shallot on its side and cut off the slices from the base. You should now have fine dice, but chop any larger pieces individually.

Spring onions

Cut off the roots and trim any coarse or withered green parts. Slice diagonally, or shred by cutting into 5cm (2in) lengths and then slicing down the lengths, or chop finely, according to the recipe.

Pak choi

Also known as bok choy, pak choi is a type of cabbage that does not form a heart. It has dark green leaves and thick fleshy white stalks, which are sometimes cooked separately.

Peeling tomatoes

1 Fill a bowl or pan with boiling water. Using a slotted spoon, add the tomato and leave for 15–30 seconds, then remove to a chopping board.

2 Use a small sharp knife to cut out the core in a single cone-shaped piece. Discard the core.

3 Peel off the skin; it should come away easily depending on ripeness.

Seeding tomatoes

1 Halve the tomato through the core. Use a spoon or a small sharp knife to remove the seeds and juice. Shake off the excess liquid.

2 Chop the tomato as required for your recipe and place in a colander for a minute or two, to drain off any excess liquid.

Cutting aubergines

1 Trim the aubergine to remove the stalk and end.

2 **Slicing** Cut the aubergine lengthways into slices as thick as the pieces you will need for your recipe.

3 **Cutting and dicing** Stack the slices and cut across them to the appropriate size for fingers. Cut in the opposite direction for dice.

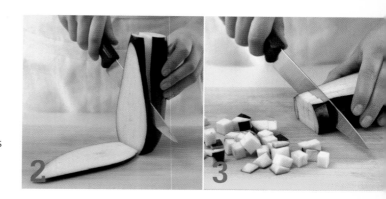

Peeling and cutting squash

1 For steaming, baking or roasting, keep the chunks fairly large – at least 2.5cm (1in) thick. Peel with a swivel-handled peeler or a chef's knife.

2 Cut the squash in half lengthways, then use a small knife to cut through some of the fibrous mass connecting the seeds with the wall of the central cavity. Scoop out the seeds and fibres with a spoon, then cut the flesh into pieces.

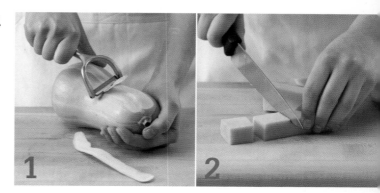

Seeding peppers

The seeds and white pith of red, green and yellow peppers taste bitter so should be removed.

1 Cut off the top of the pepper, then cut away and discard the seeds and white pith.

2 Alternatively, cut the pepper in half vertically and snap out the white pithy core and seeds. Trim away the rest of the white membrane with a knife.

Cooking beans

1 Pick through the beans to remove any grit or stones. Put the beans in a bowl or pan and pour over cold water to cover generously. Leave to soak for at least 8 hours, then drain. (Or pour boiling water over and leave the beans to cool in the water for 1–2 hours.)

2 Put the soaked beans in a large pan and add cold water to cover by at least 5cm (2in). Bring to the boil and boil rapidly for 10 minutes.

3 Skim off the scum that rises to the top, turn down the heat and leave to simmer until the beans are soft inside. They should be tender but not falling apart. Check periodically to make sure there's enough water to keep the beans well covered. Drain well. If using in a salad, allow to cool completely.

Using beans and lentils

Many dried beans and peas need to be soaked overnight before cooking. Lentils do not need soaking and are quicker to cook. Quicker still are canned beans: they are ready to use, but should be drained in a sieve and rinsed in cold water first.

Cooking times

Older beans take longer to cook, so check their 'best before' date. For some pulses, such as red kidney beans, aduki beans, black-eyed beans, black beans and borlotti beans, it is essential to cover them with fresh cold water, bring to the boil and boil rapidly for 10 minutes to destroy any toxins. Then you can reduce the heat and and cook at a steady simmer for the following times:

Chickpeas	1–2 hours
Cannellini, borlotti, butter, flageolet, red kidney beans	1–3 hours
Red lentils	20 minutes
Green lentils	30–40 minutes

Preparing prawns and mussels

Raw prawns can be cooked in or out of their shells. Large prawns may need deveining, or they will be gritty.

Peeling prawns

1 To shell prawns, pull off the head and put to one side (it can be used later for making stock). Using pointed scissors, cut through the soft shell on the belly side.

2 Prise the shell off, leaving the tail attached. (Put the shell to one side, with the head.)

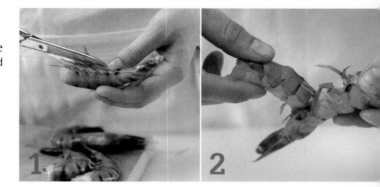

Deveining prawns

1 Using a small sharp knife, make a shallow cut along the length of the back of the prawn.

2 Using the point of the knife, carefully remove and discard the black vein (the intestinal tract) that runs along the back of the prawn.

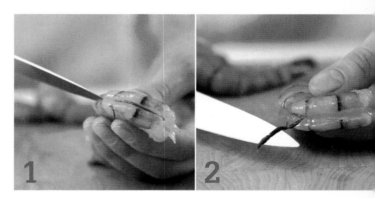

Cleaning mussels

1 Scrape off the fibres attached to the shells (beards). If the mussels are very clean, give them a quick rinse under the cold tap. If they are very sandy, scrub them with a stiff brush.

Making stock

Good stock can make the difference between a good dish and a great one. It gives depth of flavour to many dishes. There are four main types of stock: vegetable, meat, chicken and fish.

Cook's Tips

- To get a clearer liquid when making fish, meat or poultry stock, strain the cooked stock through four layers of muslin in a sieve.
- Stock will keep for three days in the refrigerator. If you want to keep it for a further three days, transfer it to a pan and reboil gently for 5 minutes. Cool, put in a clean bowl and chill for a further three days.
- When making meat or chicken stock, make sure there is a good ratio of meat to bones. The more meat you use, the more flavour the stock will have.

Stocks

Vegetable Stock

For 1.2 litres (2 pints), you will need:
225g (8oz) each onions, celery, leeks and carrots, chopped, 2 bay leaves, a few thyme sprigs, 1 small bunch parsley, 10 black peppercorns, ½ tsp salt.

1 Put all the ingredients in a large pan and add 1.7 litres (3 pints) cold water. Bring slowly to the boil and skim the surface.

2 Partially cover the pan and simmer for 30 minutes. Adjust the seasoning if necessary. Strain the stock through a fine sieve into a bowl and leave to cool.

Meat Stock

For 900ml (1½ pints), you will need:
450g (1lb) each meat bones and stewing meat, 1 onion, 2 celery sticks and 1 large carrot, sliced, 1 bouquet garni (2 bay leaves, a few thyme sprigs and a small bunch parsley), 1 tsp black peppercorns, ½ tsp salt.

1 Preheat the oven to 220°C (200°C fan oven) mark 7. Put the meat and bones in a roasting tin and roast for 30–40 minutes, turning now and again, until they are well browned.

2 Put the bones in a large pan with the remaining ingredients and add 2 litres (3½ pints) cold water. Bring slowly to the boil and skim the surface.

3 Partially cover the pan and simmer for 4–5 hours. Adjust the seasoning if necessary. Strain through a muslin-lined sieve into a bowl and cool quickly. Degrease the stock (see opposite) before using.

Chicken Stock

For 1.2 litres (2 pints), you will need:
1.6kg (3½lb) chicken bones, 225g (8oz) each onions and celery, sliced, 150g (5oz) chopped leeks, 1 bouquet garni (2 bay leaves, a few thyme sprigs and a small bunch parsley), 1 tsp black peppercorns, ½ tsp salt.

1 Put all the ingredients in a large pan and add 3 litres (5¼ pints) cold water. Bring slowly to the boil and skim the surface.

2 Partially cover the pan and simmer gently for 2 hours. Adjust the seasoning if necessary.

3 Strain the stock through a muslin-lined sieve into a bowl and cool quickly. Degrease the stock (see right) before using.

Fish Stock

For 900ml (1½ pints), you will need:
900g (2lb) fish bones and trimmings, washed, 2 carrots, 1 onion and 2 celery sticks, sliced, 1 bouquet garni (2 bay leaves, a few thyme sprigs and a small bunch parsley), 6 white peppercorns, ½ tsp salt.

1 Put all the ingredients in a large pan and add 900ml (1½ pints) cold water. Bring slowly to the boil and skim the surface.

2 Partially cover the pan and simmer gently for 30 minutes. Adjust the seasoning if necessary.

3 Strain through a muslin-lined sieve into a bowl and cool quickly. Fish stock tends not to have much fat in it and so does not usually need to be degreased. However, if it does seem to be fatty, you will need to remove this by degreasing it (see right).

Degreasing stock

Meat and poultry stock needs to be degreased. (Vegetable stock does not.) You can mop the fat from the surface using kitchen paper, but the following methods are easier and more effective. There are three main methods that you can use: ladling, pouring and chilling.

1 **Ladling** While the stock is warm, place a ladle on the surface. Press down and allow the fat floating on the surface to trickle over the edge until the ladle is full. Discard the fat, then repeat until all the fat has been removed.

2 **Pouring** For this you need a degreasing jug or a double-pouring gravy boat, which has the spout at the base of the vessel. When you fill the jug or gravy boat with a fatty liquid, the fat rises. When you pour, the stock comes out while the fat stays behind in the jug.

3 **Chilling** This technique works best with stock made from meat, as the fat solidifies when cold. Put the stock in the refrigerator until the fat becomes solid, then remove the pieces of fat using a slotted spoon.

Cooking noodles and rice

Noodles and rice are the staples of Asian cooking. Often served as an accompaniment to stir-fried dishes, they can also be cooked and added as one of the ingredients.

Perfect noodles

Use 50–75g (2–3oz) uncooked noodles per person.
Dried egg noodles are often packed in layers. As a general rule, allow one layer per person for a main dish.
If you plan to re-cook the noodles after the initial boiling or soaking – for example, in a stir-fry – it's best to undercook them slightly.
When cooking a layer, block or nest of noodles, use a fork or pair of chopsticks to untangle the strands from the moment they go into the water.

Cooking noodles

Egg (wheat) noodles

These are the most versatile of Asian noodles. Like Italian pasta, they are made from wheat flour, egg and water and are available fresh or dried in various thicknesses.

1 Bring a pan of water to the boil and put the noodles in.

2 Agitate the noodles using chopsticks or a fork to separate them. This can take a minute or even more.

3 Continue boiling for 4–5 minutes until the noodles are cooked al dente: tender but with a little bite in the centre.

4 Drain well and then rinse in cold water and toss with a little oil if you are not using them immediately.

Glass, cellophane or bean thread noodles

These very thin noodles are made from mung beans; they need only 1 minute in boiling water.

Rice noodles

These may be very fine (rice vermicelli) or thick and flat. Most need no cooking, only soaking in warm or hot water; check the packet instructions, or cover the noodles with freshly boiled water and soak until they are al dente: tender but with a little bite in the centre. Drain well and toss with a little oil if you are not using them immediately.

Cooking rice

There are two main types of rice: long-grain and short-grain. Long-grain rice is generally served as an accompaniment; the most commonly used type of long-grain rice in South-east Asian cooking is jasmine rice, also known as Thai fragrant rice. It has a distinctive taste and slightly sticky texture. Long-grain rice needs no special preparation, although it should be washed to remove excess starch. Put the rice in a bowl and cover with cold water. Stir until this becomes cloudy, then drain and repeat until the water is clear.

Long-grain rice

1 Use 50–75g (2–3oz) raw rice per person; measured by volume 50–75ml (2–2½fl oz). Measure the rice by volume and put it in a pan with a pinch of salt and twice its volume of boiling water (or stock).

2 Bring to the boil. Turn the heat down to low and set the timer for the time stated on the packet. The rice should be al dente: tender with a bite at the centre.

3 When the rice is cooked, fluff up the grains with a fork.

Basmati rice

Put the rice in a bowl and cover with cold water. Stir until this becomes cloudy, then drain and repeat until the water is clear. Soak the rice for 30 minutes, then drain before cooking for the time stated on the packet.

Perfect rice

Use 50–75g (2–3oz) raw rice per person – or measure by volume 50–75ml (2–2½fl oz).
If you cook rice often, you may want to invest in a special rice steamer. They are available in Asian supermarkets and some kitchen shops and give good, consistent results.

Accompaniments

Saffron Rice

To serve 8, you will need:
500g (1lb 2oz) basmati rice, 900ml (1½ pints) stock made with 1½ chicken stock cubes, 5 tbsp sunflower or light vegetable oil, ½ tsp saffron, salt, 75g (3oz) blanched almonds and pistachio nuts, coarsely chopped, to garnish (optional).

1 Put the rice into a bowl and cover with warm water, then drain well through a sieve.

2 Put the stock, oil and a good pinch of salt into a pan, then cover and bring to the boil. Add the saffron and the rice.

3 Cover the pan and bring the stock back to the boil, then stir, reduce the heat to low, replace the lid and cook gently for 10 minutes until little holes appear all over the surface of the cooked rice and the grains are tender. Leave to stand, covered, for 15 minutes.

4 Fluff up the rice with a fork and transfer it to a warmed serving dish. Sprinkle the nuts on top of the rice, if using, and serve.

Pilau Rice

To serve 4, you will need:
50g (2oz) butter, plus a generous knob to serve, 225g (8oz) long-grain white rice, 750ml (1¼ pints) hot chicken stock, salt and pepper.

1 Melt the butter in a pan, add the rice and fry gently for 3–4 minutes until translucent.

2 Slowly pour in the hot stock, season, stir and cover with a tight-fitting lid. Leave undisturbed over a very low heat for about 10 minutes until the water has been absorbed and the rice is just tender.

3 Remove the lid and cover the surface of the rice with a clean cloth. Replace the lid and leave to stand in a warm place for about 15 minutes to dry the rice before serving.

4 Fork through and add a knob of butter to serve.

Thai Rice

To serve 6, you will need:
500g (1lb 2oz) Thai rice, handful of mint leaves, salt.

1 Cook the rice and mint in lightly salted boiling water for 10–12 minutes or until tender. Drain well and serve.

Coconut Rice

To serve 8, you will need:
25g (1oz) butter, 450g (1lb) long-grain white rice, rinsed and drained, 1 tsp salt, 50g (2oz) creamed coconut, crumbled.

1 Melt the butter in a large pan, add the rice and stir to coat in butter. Add 1.2 litres (2 pints) cold water and the salt. Cover the pan and bring to the boil. Reduce the heat and simmer for 10–12 minutes (or according to the packet instructions) until all the water has been absorbed.

2 Once the rice is cooked, remove the pan from the heat. Add the creamed coconut. Cover the pan with a clean teatowel and replace the lid to allow the coconut to dissolve and the teatowel to absorb any steam. Fluff up with a fork before serving.

Fresh Mango Chutney

For 225g (8oz), you will need:
1 large ripe mango, 1 fresh green chilli, seeded, juice of 1 lime, 1/4 tsp cayenne pepper, 1/2 tsp salt.

1 Cut the mango in half lengthways, slicing either side of the large, flat stone; discard the stone. Using the point of a knife, cut parallel lines into the mango flesh, almost to the skin. Score another set of lines to cut the flesh into squares. Turn the skin inside out so that the cubes of flesh stand up, then cut these off and place in a bowl.

2 Cut the chilli into fine rings and mix with the mango cubes, lime juice, cayenne pepper and salt. Chill for 1 hour before serving. It will keep for up to two days in the refrigerator.

Spiced Pepper Chutney

For 1.6kg (3½lb), you will need:
3 red peppers and 3 green peppers, seeded and finely chopped, 450g (1lb) onions, chopped, 450g (1lb) tomatoes, peeled and chopped, 450g (1lb) cooking apples, peeled, cored and chopped, 225g (8oz) demerara sugar, 1 tsp ground allspice, 450ml (3/4 pint) malt vinegar, 1 tsp peppercorns, 1 tsp mustard seeds.

1 Place the peppers in a preserving pan or large, heavy-based pan with the onions, tomatoes, apples, sugar, allspice and vinegar. Tie the peppercorns and mustard seeds in a piece of muslin and add to the pan. Heat gently, stirring, until the sugar has dissolved. Bring to the boil and simmer, uncovered, over a medium heat for about 1½ hours, stirring occasionally, until soft, pulpy and well reduced. Remove the muslin bag.

2 Spoon the chutney into jars, cover and seal. It will keep for up to three months.

Chilli Chutney

For 900g (2lb), you will need:
900g (2lb) very ripe tomatoes, roughly chopped, 8 red chillies, seeded, 6 garlic cloves, crushed, 5cm (2in) piece fresh root ginger, grated, 1 lemongrass stalk, trimmed and outer layer removed, 1 star anise, 550g (1¼lb) golden caster sugar, 200ml (7fl oz) red wine vinegar.

1 Put half the tomatoes into a food processor or blender. Roughly chop the chillies, add to the blender with the garlic and ginger and blend to a purée. Transfer to a heavy-based pan.

2 Crush the lemongrass and cut in half. Tie the cut halves together with string, then add to the pan with the star anise, sugar and vinegar.

3 Bring the mixture to the boil, add the remaining tomatoes, then reduce the heat. Cook gently for 45–50 minutes, stirring occasionally and skimming off any foam, until the mixture has thickened and reduced slightly. Remove the star anise and lemongrass.

4 Spoon the chutney into jars, cover and seal. Chill and use within one month.

Fresh Coriander Chutney

For 275g (10oz), you will need:
100g (4oz) fresh coriander, washed and dried, 1 medium onion, roughly chopped, 2 fresh green chillies, seeded, 2.5cm (1in) piece fresh root ginger, peeled, 1 tsp salt, 2 tbsp lemon or lime juice, 1 tbsp desiccated coconut.

1 Put all the ingredients in a blender or food processor and blend until smooth.

2 Transfer to a glass or plastic bowl, cover and chill in the refrigerator. It will keep for up to one week.

Food storage and hygiene

Storing food properly and preparing it in a hygienic way is important to ensure that food remains as nutritious and flavourful as possible, and to reduce the risk of food poisoning.

Hygiene

When you are preparing food, always follow these important guidelines:

Wash your hands thoroughly before handling food and again between handling different types of food, such as raw and cooked meat and poultry. If you have any cuts or grazes on your hands, be sure to keep them covered with a waterproof plaster.

Wash down worksurfaces regularly with a mild detergent solution or multi-surface cleaner.

Use a dishwasher if available. Otherwise, wear rubber gloves for washing-up, so that the water temperature can be hotter than unprotected hands can bear. Change drying-up cloths and cleaning cloths regularly. Note that leaving dishes to drain is more hygienic than drying them with a teatowel.

Keep raw and cooked foods separate, especially meat, fish and poultry. Wash kitchen utensils in between preparing raw and cooked foods. Never put cooked or ready-to-eat foods directly on to a surface that has just had raw fish, meat or poultry on it.

Keep pets out of the kitchen if possible; or make sure they stay away from worksurfaces. Never allow animals on to worksurfaces.

Shopping

Always choose fresh ingredients in prime condition from stores and markets that have a regular turnover of stock to ensure you buy the freshest produce possible.

Make sure items are within their 'best before' or 'use by' date. (Foods with a longer shelf life have a 'best before' date; more perishable items have a 'use by' date.)

Pack frozen and chilled items in an insulated cool bag at the check-out and put them into the freezer or refrigerator as soon as you get home.

During warm weather in particular, buy perishable foods just before you return home. When packing items at the check-out, sort them according to where you will store them when you get home – the storecupboard, refrigerator, freezer, vegetable rack, fruit bowl, etc. This will make unpacking easier – and quicker.

The storecupboard

Although storecupboard ingredients will generally last a long time, correct storage is important:

Always check packaging for storage advice – even with familiar foods, because storage requirements may change if additives, sugar or salt have been reduced. Check storecupboard foods for their 'best before' or 'use by' date and do not use them if the date has passed.

Keep all food cupboards scrupulously clean and make sure food containers and packets are properly sealed.

Once opened, treat canned foods as though fresh. Always transfer the contents to a clean container, cover and keep in the refrigerator. Similarly, jars, sauce bottles and cartons should be kept chilled after opening. (Check the label for safe storage times after opening.)

Transfer dry goods such as sugar, flour, rice and pasta to moisture-proof containers. When supplies are used up, wash the container well and thoroughly dry before refilling with new supplies.

Store oils in a dark cupboard away from any heat source as heat and light can make them turn rancid and affect their colour. For the same reason, buy olive oil in dark green bottles.

Store vinegars in a cool place; they can turn bad in a warm environment.

Store dried herbs, spices and flavourings in a cool, dark cupboard or in dark jars. Buy in small quantities as their flavour will not last indefinitely.

Refrigerator storage

Fresh food needs to be kept in the cool temperature of the refrigerator to keep it in good condition and discourage the growth of harmful bacteria. Store day-to-day perishable items, such as opened jams and jellies, mayonnaise and bottled sauces, in the refrigerator along with eggs and dairy products, fruit juices, bacon, fresh and cooked meat (on separate shelves), and salads and vegetables (except potatoes, which don't suit being stored in the cold). A refrigerator should be kept at an operating temperature of 4–5°C. It is worth investing in a refrigerator thermometer to ensure the correct temperature is maintained.

To ensure your refrigerator is functioning effectively for safe food storage, follow these guidelines:

To avoid bacterial cross-contamination, store cooked and raw foods on separate shelves, putting cooked foods on the top shelf. Ensure that all items are well wrapped.

Never put hot food into the refrigerator, as this will cause the internal temperature of the refrigerator to rise.

Avoid overfilling the refrigerator, as this restricts the circulation of air and prevents the appliance from working properly.

It can take some time for the refrigerator to return to the correct operating temperature once the door has been opened, so don't leave it open any longer than is necessary.

Clean the refrigerator regularly, using a specially formulated germicidal refrigerator cleaner. Alternatively, use a weak solution of bicarbonate of soda: 1 tbsp to 1 litre (1¾ pints) water.

If your refrigerator doesn't have an automatic defrost facility, defrost regularly.

Maximum refrigerator storage times

For pre-packed foods, always adhere to the 'use by' date on the packet. For other foods the following storage times should apply, providing the food is in prime condition when it goes into the refrigerator and that your refrigerator is in good working order:

Vegetables

Green vegetables	3–4 days
Salad leaves	2–3 days

Dairy Food

Eggs	1 week
Milk	4–5 days

Fish

Fish	1 day
Shellfish	1 day

Raw Meat

Bacon	7 days
Game	2 days
Minced meat	1 day
Offal	1 day
Poultry	2 days
Raw sliced meat	2 days

Cooked Meat

Sliced meat	2 days
Ham	2 days
Ham, vacuum-packed (or according to the instructions on the packet)	1–2 weeks

1

Snacks and
Side Dishes

Prawn Poppadoms

24 raw tiger prawns, peeled and deveined

4 tbsp Sweet Chilli Sauce (see page 56)

½ tbsp sesame oil

150ml (¼ pint) soured cream

24 mini poppadoms

1 lime, cut into thin wedges, to serve

1 Quickly fry the prawns with 2 tbsp sweet chilli sauce and the sesame oil for 3–4 minutes until just pink.

2 Mix the remaining sweet chilli sauce with the soured cream, then spoon on to the poppadoms. Top each with a prawn and a sliver of fresh lime (assemble just before serving, otherwise the poppadoms will go soft).

	EASY		NUTRITIONAL INFORMATION	
Makes 24	Preparation Time 10 minutes	Cooking Time 3 minutes	Per Serving 57 calories, 3.1g fat (of which 1.1g saturates), 4.2g carbohydrate, 0.2g salt	Gluten free

Try Something Different

Replace the goat's cheese with two roasted, skinless chicken breasts, which have been shredded.

½ tbsp ground cumin

½ tsp ground cinnamon

2 tbsp sunflower oil

2 large red onions, sliced

250g (9oz) basmati rice

600ml (1 pint) hot vegetable or chicken stock

400g can lentils, drained and rinsed

salt and ground black pepper

For the salad

75g (3oz) watercress

250g (9oz) broccoli, steamed and chopped into 2.5cm (1in) pieces

25g (1oz) sultanas

75g (3oz) dried apricots, chopped

75g (3oz) mixed nuts and seeds

2 tbsp freshly chopped flat-leafed parsley

100g (3½oz) goat's cheese, crumbled

Warm Spiced Rice Salad

1 Put the cumin and cinnamon into a large, deep frying pan and heat gently for 1–2 minutes. Add the oil and onions and fry over a low heat for 8–10 minutes until the onions are soft. Add the rice, toss to coat in the spices and onions, then add the stock. Cover and cook for 12–15 minutes until the stock has been absorbed and the rice is cooked. Season, tip into a serving bowl and add the lentils.

2 To make the salad, add the watercress, broccoli, sultanas, apricots and mixed nuts and seeds to the bowl. Scatter with the parsley, then toss together, top with the cheese and serve immediately.

EASY		NUTRITIONAL INFORMATION		Serves
Preparation Time 10 minutes	**Cooking Time** 20–30 minutes	**Per Serving** 700 calories, 27g fat (of which 6g saturates), 88g carbohydrate, 0.7g salt	Vegetarian Gluten free	**4**

Thai Crab Balls with Sweet Chilli Sauce

2 tsp sesame oil

1 large red chilli, seeded and finely chopped (see page 38)

2.5cm (1in) piece fresh root ginger, peeled and finely grated, plus 2 tbsp finely chopped fresh root ginger

2 garlic cloves, crushed

8 tbsp light muscovado sugar

3 tsp Thai fish sauce

2 tbsp light soy sauce

juice of 2 limes

1 tbsp sunflower oil, plus extra for deep-frying

4 spring onions, finely chopped

1 lemongrass stalk, outer leaves discarded and remainder finely chopped

350g (12oz) fresh or frozen crabmeat

2 tbsp freshly chopped coriander

75g (3oz) white breadcrumbs

3 medium eggs

ground black pepper

50g (2oz) plain flour

coriander sprigs, shredded red chilli and lime wedges to garnish

1 To make the sweet chilli sauce, put the sesame oil in a pan and heat gently. Add ½ tsp chopped chilli, 2 tbsp chopped ginger and 1 garlic clove and cook for 1–2 minutes until softened. Add the sugar, 2 tsp fish sauce and the soy sauce, then bring to the boil, reduce the heat and simmer for 2 minutes. Remove from the heat and stir in 8 tbsp water and the lime juice. Pour into a serving bowl, cover and put to one side.

2 To make the crab balls, heat 1 tbsp sunflower oil in a small pan and add the spring onions, the grated ginger, remaining chilli and garlic and the lemongrass. Cook gently for 2–3 minutes until soft. Transfer to a bowl and cool, then stir in the crabmeat, coriander, remaining fish sauce, 6 tbsp breadcrumbs and 1 egg. Mix and season with pepper only. Shape tablespoonfuls of the mixture into 18 balls, put on a baking sheet and chill for 20 minutes.

3 Beat the remaining eggs. Coat each ball lightly with flour, roll them in the beaten eggs, then in the remaining breadcrumbs. Heat the sunflower oil in a large pan and deep-fry the crab balls in batches for 3–4 minutes or until golden. Drain on kitchen paper and keep warm while frying the remaining balls. Garnish with coriander sprigs, shredded red chilli and lime wedges and serve with the sweet chilli sauce.

A LITTLE EFFORT		NUTRITIONAL INFORMATION		Makes **18** balls
Preparation Time 30 minutes, plus chilling	**Cooking Time** 20 minutes	**Per Ball with Sauce** 127 calories, 6.8g fat (of which 1g saturates), 11.1g carbohydrate, 0.8g salt	Dairy free	

Get Ahead

To prepare ahead, fry the aubergine and onion as in step 1. Cover and keep in a cool place for 1½ hours.
To use Complete the recipe.

Aubergine and Chickpea Pilaf

4–6 tbsp olive oil

275g (10oz) aubergine, roughly chopped

225g (8oz) onions, finely chopped

25g (1oz) butter

½ tsp cumin seeds

175g (6oz) long-grain rice

600ml (1 pint) vegetable or chicken stock

400g can chickpeas, drained and rinsed

225g (8oz) baby spinach leaves

salt and ground black pepper

1 Heat half the oil in a large pan or flameproof casserole over a medium heat. Fry the aubergine for 4–5 minutes, in batches, until deep golden brown. Remove from the pan with a slotted spoon and put to one side. Add the remaining oil to the pan, then add the onions and cook for 5 minutes or until golden and soft.

2 Add the butter, then stir in the cumin seeds and rice. Fry for 1–2 minutes. Pour in the stock, season with salt and pepper and bring to the boil. Reduce the heat, then simmer, uncovered, for 10–12 minutes until most of the liquid has evaporated and the rice is tender.

3 Remove the pan from the heat. Stir in the chickpeas, spinach and reserved aubergine. Cover with a tight-fitting lid and leave to stand for 5 minutes until the spinach has wilted and the chickpeas are heated through. Adjust the seasoning to taste. Fork through the rice grains to separate and make the rice fluffy before serving.

Serves 4	EASY		NUTRITIONAL INFORMATION	
	Preparation Time 10 minutes	**Cooking Time** 20 minutes, plus 5 minutes standing	**Per Serving** 462 calories, 20g fat (of which 5g saturates), 58g carbohydrate, 0.9g salt	Vegetarian Gluten free

Cook's Tip

For a lower-fat version of this recipe, bake the goujons in the oven. Preheat the oven to 200°C (180°C fan oven) mark 6. Put the goujons on a lightly oiled baking sheet, brush each with a little oil and bake for 12–15 minutes until golden and cooked through.

Lime and Chilli Chicken Goujons

300g (11oz) boneless, skinless chicken thighs
50g (2oz) fresh breadcrumbs
50g (2oz) plain flour
2 tsp dried chilli flakes
grated zest of 1 lime
1 tsp salt
1 medium egg, beaten
2 tbsp sunflower oil
lime wedges to serve

For the dip

6 tbsp natural yogurt
6 tbsp mayonnaise
¼ cucumber, halved, seeded and finely diced
25g (1oz) freshly chopped coriander
juice of 1 lime
salt and ground black pepper

1 Put all the ingredients for the dip into a bowl. Season with salt and pepper and mix well, then chill.

2 Cut the chicken into strips. Put the breadcrumbs into a bowl with the flour, chilli flakes, lime zest and salt. Mix well. Pour the egg on to a plate. Dip the chicken strips in egg, then coat in the breadcrumb mixture.

3 Heat the oil in a frying pan over a medium heat. Fry the chicken in batches for 7–10 minutes until golden and cooked through. Keep warm while cooking the remainder. Transfer to a serving plate, sprinkle with a little salt, then serve with the dip and lime wedges.

EASY		NUTRITIONAL INFORMATION	Serves
Preparation Time 15 minutes	**Cooking Time** 20 minutes	**Per Serving** 420 calories, 28.7g fat (of which 5g saturates), 21.9g carbohydrate, 2g salt	**4**

Cook's Tips

Chillies vary enormously in strength, from quite mild to blisteringly hot, depending on the type of chilli and its ripeness. Taste a small piece first to check that it's not too hot for you.

When handling chillies, be extremely careful not to touch or rub your eyes with your fingers, as it will make them sting. Wash knives immediately after chopping chillies. As a precaution, use rubber gloves when preparing them if you like.

Bean Sprouts with Peppers and Chillies

3 tbsp vegetable oil

2 garlic cloves, chopped

2.5cm (1in) piece fresh root ginger, peeled and chopped

6 spring onions, cut into 2.5cm (1in) pieces

1 red pepper, seeded and thinly sliced

1 yellow pepper, seeded and thinly sliced

2 green chillies, seeded and finely chopped (see Cook's Tips)

350g (12oz) bean sprouts

1 tbsp dark soy sauce

1 tbsp sugar

1 tbsp malt vinegar

a few drops of sesame oil (optional)

boiled rice with 2 tbsp freshly chopped coriander stirred through to serve

1 Heat the oil in a wok or large frying pan. Add the garlic, ginger, spring onions, peppers, chillies and bean sprouts and stir-fry over a medium heat for 3 minutes.

2 Add the soy sauce, sugar and vinegar and fry, stirring, for a further minute.

3 Sprinkle with a few drops of sesame oil, if you like, then serve immediately with coriander rice.

Serves	EASY		NUTRITIONAL INFORMATION	
4	**Preparation Time** 10 minutes	**Cooking Time** 4 minutes	**Per Serving** 149 calories, 9g fat (of which 1g saturates), 14g carbohydrate, 0.7g salt	Vegetarian • Dairy free

4 tbsp olive oil

4 tsp lime juice

large pinch of golden caster sugar

50g (2oz) chorizo sausage, thinly shredded

2 mild red chillies, seeded and chopped (see page 38)

2 red peppers, seeded and sliced

2 shallots, finely chopped

4 tomatoes, chopped

large bag mixed crisp lettuce leaves

salt and crushed black peppercorns

wholemeal rolls or rye bread to serve

Spiced Salad

1 Put the oil, lime juice, sugar, some salt and crushed black peppercorns into a bowl and stir to combine.

2 Add the chorizo sausage, chillies, red peppers, shallots, tomatoes and lettuce leaves and turn in the dressing.

3 Serve with wholemeal rolls or slices of rye bread.

EASY	NUTRITIONAL INFORMATION		Serves
Preparation Time 5 minutes	**Per Serving** 210 calories, 17.4g fat (of which 1.8g saturates), 9.6g carbohydrate, 0.6g salt	Gluten free • Dairy free	**4**

Split Pea Roti

125g (4oz) yellow split peas, soaked in
cold water overnight

¼ tsp ground turmeric

1 tsp ground cumin

1 garlic clove, finely sliced

1½ tsp salt

225g (8oz) plain flour, plus extra to dust

1½ tsp baking powder

1 tbsp vegetable oil, plus extra to fry

125–150ml (4–5fl oz) full-fat milk

vegetable curry to serve

1 Drain the split peas and put into a small pan with the turmeric, cumin, garlic and 1 tsp salt. Add 200ml (7fl oz) cold water and bring to the boil, then reduce the heat and simmer for 30 minutes or until the peas are soft, adding a little more water if necessary. Take off the heat and leave to cool.

2 Sift the flour, baking powder and remaining salt into a large bowl. Make a well in the centre, add the oil and gradually mix in enough milk to form a soft dough. Transfer to a lightly floured surface and knead until smooth. Cover with a damp teatowel and leave to rest for 30 minutes.

3 Put the cooled peas in a food processor and blend until smooth, adding 1 tbsp water.

4 Divide the dough into eight. Roll out each piece on a lightly floured surface, to make a 20cm (8in) round. Divide the pea mixture between four of the rounds, placing it in the centre, then top with the other rounds and press the edges together to seal.

5 Heat a large heavy-based frying pan until really hot. Brush each roti with a little oil and fry (one or two at a time) for 1 minute on each side or until lightly brown. Keep warm while you cook the rest. Serve with a vegetable curry.

EASY		NUTRITIONAL INFORMATION		Serves
Preparation Time 25 minutes, plus soaking and resting	**Cooking Time** 40 minutes	**Per Serving** 429 calories, 13.7g fat (of which 2g saturates), 65.5g carbohydrate, 1.3g salt	Vegetarian	**4**

Chilli-roasted Nuts and Raisins

220g pack mixed unsalted nuts, seeds and raisins (not roasted)

1 tsp ground paprika

a large pinch of dried crushed chilli flakes

2 tsp olive oil

fine sea salt

1 Preheat the oven to 200°C (180°C fan oven) mark 6. Put the nuts, seeds and raisins in a small bowl and stir in the paprika, chilli flakes and oil.

2 Tip the nuts on to an edged baking sheet and season lightly with salt. Roast in the oven, stirring occasionally, for 12–15 minutes until golden and toasted. Serve warm or cool. Store in an airtight container; they will keep for up to five days.

Serves 6	EASY		NUTRITIONAL INFORMATION	
	Preparation Time 3 minutes	**Cooking Time** 12–15 minutes	**Per Serving** 169 calories, 11g fat (of which 2g saturates), 14g carbohydrate, 0.2g salt	Vegetarian Gluten free • Dairy free

Get Ahead

Make up to the end of step 2, up to a day ahead. Cover and chill the rice and onions separately.
To serve Complete the recipe.

3 tbsp olive oil

1 large red onion, thinly sliced

1 red chilli, seeded and thinly sliced (see page 38)

1 tbsp tamarind paste

1 tbsp light muscovado sugar

350g (12oz) mixed basmati and wild rice

a little oil or butter to grease

20g pack fresh mint, roughly chopped

100g bag baby leaf spinach

50g (2oz) flaked almonds, toasted

salt and ground black pepper

Oven-baked Chilli Rice

1 Heat the oil in a frying pan and fry the onion for 7–10 minutes over a medium heat until golden and soft. Add the chilli, tamarind paste and sugar. Cool, cover and chill.

2 Meanwhile, put the rice in a large pan. Add 800ml (1 pint 7fl oz) boiling water. Cover and bring to the boil, then turn the heat to its lowest setting and cook according to the packet instructions. Spread on a baking sheet and leave to cool, then chill.

3 When ready to serve, preheat the oven to 200°C (180°C fan oven) mark 6. Tip the rice into a lightly greased, shallow ovenproof dish. Stir in the onion mixture and season with salt and pepper.

4 Reheat the rice in the oven for 20 minutes until piping hot. Stir in the mint, spinach and almonds and serve immediately.

EASY		NUTRITIONAL INFORMATION		Serves
Preparation Time 15 minutes, plus chilling	**Cooking Time** 40 minutes	**Per Serving** 265 calories, 8.1g fat (of which 0.9g saturates), 42.2g carbohydrate, 0.1g salt	Vegetarian Gluten free • Dairy free	**8**

Chilli Onions with Goat's Cheese

75g (3oz) unsalted butter, softened

2 medium red chillies, seeded and finely chopped (see page 38)

1 tsp crushed dried chillies

6 small red onions

3 x 100g (3½oz) goat's cheese logs, with rind

salt and ground black pepper

balsamic vinegar to serve

1 Preheat the oven to 200°C (180°C fan oven) mark 6. Put the butter in a small bowl, beat in the fresh and dried chillies and season well with salt and pepper.

2 Cut off the root from one of the onions, sit it on its base, then make several deep cuts in the top to create a star shape, slicing about two-thirds of the way down the onion. Do the same with the other five onions, then divide the chilli butter equally among them, pushing it down into the cuts.

3 Put the onions in a small roasting tin, cover with foil and bake for 40–45 minutes until soft. About 5 minutes before they are ready, slice each goat's cheese in two, leaving the rind intact, then put on a baking sheet and bake for 2–3 minutes. To serve, put each onion on top of a piece of goat's cheese and drizzle with balsamic vinegar.

Serves 6	EASY		NUTRITIONAL INFORMATION	
	Preparation Time 15 minutes	Cooking Time 45 minutes	Per Serving 276 calories, 23g fat (of which 16g saturates), 5g carbohydrate, 0.9g salt	Vegetarian Gluten free

Get Ahead

Complete the recipe, store in an airtight container and chill. It will keep for up to one day.

Melon, Mango and Cucumber Salad

½ cucumber, halved lengthways and seeded

1 Charentais melon, halved and seeded

1 mango, peeled and stoned

freshly chopped flat-leafed parsley and lime wedges to serve

For the wasabi dressing

3 tsp tamari or light soy sauce

1 tbsp dry sherry

1 tbsp rice wine vinegar or white wine vinegar

¼ tsp wasabi paste or finely chopped green chilli

1 Cut the cucumber into slim diagonal slices. Cut the rind off the melon and cut the flesh into pieces that are a similar size to the cucumber slices. Cut the mango flesh into similar-sized lengths. Mix the cucumber, melon and mango in a large bowl.

2 Whisk all the ingredients for the wasabi dressing in a small bowl, then pour over the salad and toss gently. Sprinkle with chopped flat-leafed parsley and serve with lime wedges.

EASY	**NUTRITIONAL INFORMATION**		**Serves**
Preparation Time 15 minutes, plus chilling	**Per Serving** 62 calories, trace fat, 14g carbohydrate, 1.5g salt	Vegetarian Dairy free	**6**

Saag Aloo

2–3 tbsp vegetable oil

1 onion, finely sliced

2 garlic cloves, finely chopped

1 tbsp black mustard seeds

2 tsp ground turmeric

900g (2lb) potatoes, peeled and cut into 4cm (½in) chunks

1 tsp salt

4 handfuls baby spinach leaves

1 Heat the oil in a pan and fry the onion over a medium heat for 10 minutes until golden, taking care not to burn it.

2 Add the garlic, mustard seeds and turmeric and cook for 1 minute. Add the potatoes, salt and 150ml (¼ pint) water. Cover the pan, bring to the boil, then reduce the heat and cook gently for 35–40 minutes or until tender. Add the spinach and cook until the leaves just wilt. Serve immediately.

Serves 4	EASY		NUTRITIONAL INFORMATION	
	Preparation Time 15 minutes	**Cooking Time** 55 minutes	**Per Serving** 295 calories, 10.2g fat (of which 1.2g saturates), 46.7g carbohydrate, 0.2g salt	Vegetarian Gluten free • Dairy free

2

Light Bites

Chicken Fajitas

4 skinless chicken breasts, about 700g (1½lb) total
weight, cut into chunky strips

2 tbsp fajita seasoning

1 tbsp sunflower oil

1 red pepper, seeded and sliced

360g jar fajita sauce

1 bunch of spring onions, trimmed and halved

8 large flour tortillas

150g (5oz) tomato salsa

125g (4oz) guacamole dip

150ml (¼ pint) soured cream

1 Put the chicken breasts in a shallow dish and toss with the fajita seasoning. Heat the oil in a large non-stick frying pan, add the chicken and cook for 5 minutes or until golden brown and tender.

2 Add the red pepper and cook for 2 minutes. Pour in the fajita sauce, bring to the boil and simmer for 5 minutes or until thoroughly heated. Add a splash of boiling water if the sauce becomes too thick. Stir in the spring onions and cook for 2 minutes.

3 Meanwhile, warm the tortillas in a microwave on full power for 45 seconds, or wrap in foil and warm in a preheated oven at 180°C (160°C fan oven) mark 4 for 10 minutes.

4 Transfer the chicken to a serving dish and take to the table, along with the tortillas, salsa, guacamole and soured cream. Let everyone help themselves.

Serves	EASY		NUTRITIONAL INFORMATION
4	**Preparation Time** 10 minutes	**Cooking Time** 10 minutes	**Per Serving** 651 calories, 23g fat (of which 8g saturates), 63g carbohydrate, 1.6g salt

2 tbsp sunflower oil

225g (8oz) fillet steak, cut into thin strips

1.2 litres (2 pints) beef stock

2–3 tbsp Thai fish sauce

1 large red chilli, seeded and finely sliced (see page 38)

1 lemongrass stalk, trimmed and thinly sliced

2.5cm (1in) piece fresh root ginger, peeled and finely shredded

6 spring onions, halved lengthways and cut into 2.5cm (1in) lengths

1 garlic clove, crushed

¼ tsp caster sugar

15g (½oz) dried porcini or shiitake mushrooms, broken into pieces and soaked in 150ml (¼ pint) boiling water for 15 minutes

50g (2oz) medium egg noodles

125g (4oz) spinach leaves, roughly chopped

4 tbsp freshly chopped coriander

salt and ground black pepper

Spiced Beef and Noodle Soup

1 Heat the oil in a large pan, then brown the meat in two batches and put to one side.

2 Pour the stock into the pan with 2 tbsp fish sauce, the chilli, lemongrass, ginger, spring onions, garlic and sugar. Add the mushrooms and their soaking liquid. Bring the mixture to the boil.

3 Break up the noodles slightly and add them to the pan, then stir gently until they begin to separate. Simmer the soup, stirring occasionally, for 4–5 minutes until the noodles are just tender.

4 Stir in the spinach and coriander. Season with salt and pepper and add the remaining fish sauce to taste, then divide the soup among four. Add some beef to each bowl and serve immediately.

EASY		NUTRITIONAL INFORMATION		Serves
Preparation Time 20 minutes	**Cooking Time** 15 minutes	**Per Serving** 215 calories, 13g fat (of which 3g saturates), 11g carbohydrate, 1.2g salt	Dairy free	**4**

Cook's Tip

Thai red curry paste is a hot chilli paste; if you prefer a milder version, use Thai green curry paste.

Hot and Sour Turkey Soup

1 tbsp vegetable oil

300g (11oz) turkey breasts, cut into strips

5cm (2in) piece fresh root ginger, peeled and grated

4 spring onions, finely sliced

1–2 tbsp Thai red curry paste

75g (3oz) basmati rice

1.2 litres (2 pints) weak hot chicken or vegetable stock, or boiling water

200g (7oz) mangetouts, sliced

juice of 1 lime

1 Heat the oil in a deep pan. Add the turkey and cook over a medium heat for 5 minutes until browned.

2 Add the ginger and spring onions. Cook for a further 2–3 minutes. Stir in the curry paste and cook for 1–2 minutes to warm the spices.

3 Add the rice and stir to coat in the curry paste. Pour the hot stock into the pan, stir once and bring to the boil. Turn down the heat and leave to simmer, covered, for 20 minutes.

4 Add the mangetouts and simmer for 1–2 minutes, then stir in the lime juice before serving.

Serves 4	EASY		NUTRITIONAL INFORMATION	
	Preparation Time 15 minutes	**Cooking Time** 40 minutes	**Per Serving** 217 calories, 6.5g fat (of which 0.8g saturates), 18.4g carbohydrate, 0.1g salt	Gluten free • Dairy free

Cook's Tip

Caesar Dressing: put 1 egg, 1 garlic clove, juice of ½ lemon, 2 tsp Dijon mustard and 1 tsp balsamic vinegar in a food processor and mix until smooth, then, with the motor running, gradually add 150ml (¼ pint) sunflower oil and blend until smooth. Season with salt and pepper, cover and chill. It will keep for up to three days.

Warm Spiced Salmon Niçoise

350g (12oz) new potatoes, thickly sliced
175g (6oz) fine green beans, halved
175g (6oz) cherry tomatoes, halved
1 small red onion, cut into thin wedges
4 x 150–175g (5–6oz) salmon fillets, skinned
15g (½oz) butter, melted
1 tbsp coriander seeds, crushed
½ tsp dried crushed chillies
4 tbsp Caesar Dressing (see Cook's Tip)
flaked sea salt and ground black pepper
fresh chives to garnish

1 Cook the potatoes in lightly salted boiling water for 8–10 minutes until just tender, adding the beans for the last 2 minutes. Drain well, then transfer to a bowl with the tomatoes and onion wedges.

2 Cut each salmon fillet into three strips. Place the strips in four piles on a baking sheet and brush each pile with the melted butter. Mix the crushed coriander seeds with the chillies and a little sea salt and sprinkle evenly over the salmon. Place under a hot grill for 4–5 minutes until just cooked through.

3 Add 1 tbsp water to the Caesar dressing to thin it slightly (it should be the consistency of single cream). Spoon three-quarters of the dressing over the vegetables and toss to coat. Season well.

4 Divide the vegetables among four plates, top with the salmon and drizzle the remaining dressing around the edge of the salad. Garnish with chives and serve.

EASY		NUTRITIONAL INFORMATION		Serves
Preparation Time 15 minutes	**Cooking Time** 15 minutes	**Per Serving** 480 calories, 28g fat (of which 6g saturates), 18g carbohydrate, 0.6g salt	Gluten free	**4**

Thai Fishcakes with Chilli Mayo

1 bunch of spring onions

2.5cm (1in) piece fresh root ginger, peeled and roughly chopped

1 lemongrass stalk, roughly chopped

20g pack coriander

½ red chilli, seeded (see page 38)

1 tsp Thai fish sauce (optional)

150ml (¼ pint) mayonnaise

75g (3oz) fresh white breadcrumbs

225g (8oz) haddock

225g (8oz) cooked and peeled prawns

oil for frying

2 tbsp Thai sweet chilli sauce

20g pack basil, roughly chopped

1 fat garlic clove, crushed (optional)

strips of red chilli to garnish

2 limes, cut into wedges, and 120g bag baby leaf spinach to serve

1 Put the spring onions, ginger, lemongrass, coriander, chilli and fish sauce, if using, in a food processor and blend to a rough paste. Add 3 tbsp mayonnaise, the breadcrumbs, haddock and prawns and blend for 5 seconds.

2 With wet hands, shape the mixture into eight patties, each about 5cm (2in) in diameter.

3 Heat a drizzle of oil in a non-stick frying pan. Fry the patties in two batches for 3–4 minutes on each side until crisp and golden.

4 Mix the sweet chilli sauce, basil and garlic, if using, into the remaining mayonnaise. Serve with the fishcakes, red chilli strips, lime wedges and spinach leaves.

EASY		NUTRITIONAL INFORMATION		Serves
Preparation Time 25 minutes	**Cooking Time** 8–10 minutes	**Per Serving** 554 calories, 44g fat (of which 5.9g saturates), 17.3g carbohydrate, 1.3g salt	Dairy free	**4**

Chilli Prawns with Sweet Chilli Sauce

6 tbsp groundnut oil

200ml (7fl oz) coconut milk

2 tsp mild chilli powder

3 garlic cloves, finely chopped

30 raw prawns, peeled and deveined, with tail left on

salt and ground black pepper

For the sweet chilli sauce

1 tbsp olive oil

2 large garlic cloves, finely chopped

2 tsp tomato purée

550g (1¼lb) tomatoes, cut into chunks

4 large red chillies, seeded and finely chopped (see page 38)

200g (7oz) dark muscovado sugar

100ml (3½fl oz) white wine vinegar

1 In a large bowl, mix together the groundnut oil, coconut milk, chilli powder, garlic and ½ tsp each of salt and pepper. Add the prawns, tossing to coat evenly. Cover and marinate for at least 2 hours at room temperature or overnight in the refrigerator.

2 Meanwhile, make the chilli sauce. Heat the olive oil in a pan, add the garlic and tomato purée and cook for 30 seconds. Add the tomatoes, chillies, sugar and vinegar. Bring to the boil and bubble for 30–35 minutes until reduced and pulpy. Pour the tomato mixture into a sieve and, using the back of a ladle, push through as much of the pulp as possible. Return to the pan and simmer for 5 minutes. Add salt to taste. Set aside.

3 Preheat the barbecue or grill. Soak six wooden skewers in water for 20 minutes. Thread five prawns on each skewer and barbecue or grill for 3–4 minutes on each side, basting with the marinade. Serve with the chilli sauce, for dipping.

Serves 6	EASY		NUTRITIONAL INFORMATION	
	Preparation Time 30 minutes, plus soaking and 2 hours marinating	**Cooking Time** 50 minutes	**Per Serving** 211 calories, 4g fat (of which 1g saturates), 38g carbohydrate, 0.2g salt	Gluten free • Dairy free

2 tbsp vegetable oil

500g (1lb 2oz) shelled large scallops, cut into 5mm (¼in) slices

4 celery sticks, sliced diagonally

1 bunch of spring onions, sliced diagonally

25g (1oz) piece fresh root ginger, peeled and shredded

2 large garlic cloves, sliced

¼ tsp chilli powder

2 tbsp lemon juice

2 tbsp light soy sauce

3 tbsp freshly chopped coriander

salt and ground black pepper

rice to serve

Scallops with Ginger

1 Heat the oil in a wok or large frying pan. Add the scallops, celery, spring onions, ginger, garlic and chilli powder and stir-fry over a high heat for 2 minutes or until the vegetables are just tender.

2 Pour in the lemon juice and soy sauce, allow to bubble up, then stir in about 2 tbsp chopped coriander and season with salt and pepper. Sprinkle with the remaining coriander and serve with rice.

EASY		NUTRITIONAL INFORMATION		Serves
Preparation Time 15 minutes	**Cooking Time** 3 minutes	**Per Serving** 197 calories, 7g fat (of which 1g saturates), 6g carbohydrate, 2g salt	Dairy free	**4**

3 tbsp olive oil

75g (3oz) wholemeal breadcrumbs

1 bunch of spring onions, finely chopped

1 orange pepper, seeded and chopped

1 small green chilli, seeded and finely chopped (see page 38)

1 garlic clove, crushed

1 tsp ground turmeric (optional)

400g can mixed beans, drained and rinsed

3 tbsp mayonnaise

a small handful of fresh basil, chopped

salt and ground black pepper

soured cream, freshly chopped coriander and lime wedges to serve (optional)

Chilli Bean Cake

1 Heat 2 tbsp oil in a non-stick frying pan over a medium heat and fry the breadcrumbs until golden and beginning to crisp. Remove and put to one side.

2 Using the same pan, add the remaining oil and fry the spring onions until soft and golden. Add the orange pepper, chilli, garlic and turmeric, if using, and cook, stirring, for 5 minutes.

3 Tip in the beans, mayonnaise, two-thirds of the fried breadcrumbs and the basil. Season with salt and pepper, mash roughly with a fork, then press down the mixture to flatten it. Sprinkle with the remaining breadcrumbs. Fry the bean cake over a medium heat for 4–5 minutes until the base is golden. Remove from the heat, cut into wedges and serve with soured cream, coriander and lime wedges, if you like.

Serves 4	EASY		NUTRITIONAL INFORMATION	
	Preparation Time 10 minutes	**Cooking Time** 20 minutes	**Per Serving** 265 calories, 6g fat (of which 1g saturates), 41g carbohydrate, 2.1g salt	Vegetarian Dairy free

Teriyaki Beef Sandwich

700g (1½lb) piece beef sirloin or rump steak, trimmed of fat and sinew and sliced thickly

6 tbsp teriyaki marinade

1 tbsp sesame oil

300ml (½ pint) mayonnaise

4 tsp wasabi paste

2 ciabatta loaves, split in half lengthways

250g (9oz) baby plum tomatoes, threaded on to metal skewers

olive oil to brush

75g (3oz) fresh rocket

1 small radicchio, shredded

salt and ground black pepper

1 Place the beef in a shallow glass dish. Mix the teriyaki marinade with the sesame oil. Pour over the meat, turning to coat evenly. Cover and chill for 4 hours or overnight, turning occasionally. Mix the mayonnaise with the wasabi paste, season with salt and pepper, cover and leave in a cool place.

2 Preheat the barbecue or grill. Remove the meat from the marinade and pat dry. Cook for 15–20 minutes for medium-rare and 20–25 minutes for well done, turning frequently. Transfer to a board, cover with foil and leave to rest for 10 minutes.

3 Toast the ciabatta halves, wrap in foil and put to one side to keep warm. Brush the tomato skewers with oil and cook for 1–2 minutes on each side. Slice the beef thinly. Spread two ciabatta halves liberally with the mayonnaise mixture. Top each with rocket and radicchio, slices of beef and the tomatoes. Top with more mayonnaise and sandwich with the remaining ciabatta. Cut each loaf into three before serving.

EASY		NUTRITIONAL INFORMATION		Serves
Preparation Time 25 minutes, plus minimum 4 hours marinating	**Cooking Time** 15–25 minutes, plus resting	**Per Serving** 710 calories, 48g fat (of which 9g saturates), 37g carbohydrate, 1.7g salt	Dairy free	**6**

Crispy Duck with Hot and Sweet Dip

8 small duck legs

2 pieces star anise

4 fat garlic cloves, sliced

1 dried red chilli

grated zest and juice of 1 orange

1 tbsp tamarind juice or lemon juice

fried garlic slivers, fried chilli pieces and star anise to garnish

For the hot and sweet dip

200ml (7fl oz) white wine vinegar

150g (5oz) golden caster sugar

75g (3oz) each cucumber, spring onion and mango, cut into fine shreds

1 dried red chilli or ¼ tsp seeded and shredded red chilli (see page 38)

1 To make the hot and sweet dip, boil the vinegar and sugar together in a pan for 2 minutes, then stir in the cucumber, spring onion, mango and chilli. Transfer to a serving bowl and leave to cool.

2 Prick the duck legs all over with a skewer or fork. Put them in a large pan, cover with cold water and bring to the boil, then reduce the heat and simmer for 45 minutes.

3 Meanwhile, put the 2 star anise, garlic, chilli, orange zest and juice and tamarind or lemon juice in a blender and mix to a paste. Preheat the grill.

4 Drain the duck and put, skin-side down, on a foil-lined grill pan. Brush half the spice paste over the duck. Grill for 5 minutes, then turn skin-side up and brush the remaining paste over it. Grill for a further 5–7 minutes or until the duck skin is well charred and crisp. Garnish with the fried garlic slivers, fried chilli pieces and star anise and serve with the hot and sweet dip.

Serves 4	EASY		NUTRITIONAL INFORMATION	
	Preparation Time 10 minutes	**Cooking Time** 1 hour	**Per Serving** 504 calories, 28.4g fat (of which 6.3g saturates), 42.4g carbohydrate, 0.5g salt	Gluten free • Dairy free

Chicken Tikka with Coconut Dressing

125ml (4fl oz) crème fraîche

5 tbsp coconut milk

4 pitta breads

200g (7oz) mixed salad leaves

400g (14oz) cooked chicken tikka fillets, sliced

2 spring onions, finely sliced

2 tbsp mango chutney

15g (½oz) flaked almonds

25g (1oz) raisins

1 Mix the crème fraîche and coconut milk together in a bowl and put to one side.

2 Split each pitta bread to form a pocket, then fill with a generous handful of salad leaves. Divide the chicken among the pitta breads. Sprinkle some spring onion over the chicken, add the mango chutney and drizzle with the crème fraîche mixture. Top with a sprinkling of flaked almonds and raisins. Serve immediately.

Serves 4	EASY	NUTRITIONAL INFORMATION
	Preparation Time 10 minutes	**Per Serving** 503 calories, 19.1g fat (of which 9.9g saturates), 55.2g carbohydrate, 1.3g salt

1 tbsp olive oil

4 boneless, skinless chicken thighs, about 300g (11oz), shredded

3 garlic cloves, roughly chopped

2 red chillies, seeded and finely diced (see page 38)

1 lemongrass stalk, finely sliced

5cm (2in) piece fresh root ginger, peeled and finely chopped

150ml (¼ pint) dry white wine

1 litre (1¾ pints) chicken stock

8 fresh coriander sprigs

50g (2oz) rice noodles

125g (4oz) green beans, trimmed and halved

125g (4oz) bean sprouts

4 spring onions, finely sliced

2 tbsp Thai fish sauce

juice of ½ lime

salt and ground black pepper

Thai Chicken Broth

1 Heat the oil in a large pan over a medium heat. Add the chicken, garlic, chillies, lemongrass and ginger and cook for 3–5 minutes until the chicken is opaque. Add the wine, bring to the boil and simmer until reduced by half. Add the stock and bring to the boil, then simmer for 5 minutes or until the chicken is cooked through.

2 Pick the leaves off the coriander and put them to one side. Finely chop the coriander stalks. Add the noodles to the pan and cook for 1 minute, then add the beans and coriander stalks. Cook for 3 minutes.

3 Add the bean sprouts and spring onions (reserving a few to garnish), along with the fish sauce and lime juice. Bring to the boil and taste for seasoning. Ladle the noodles and broth into four warmed bowls, making sure that each serving has some chicken and bean sprouts. Garnish with the reserved coriander leaves, spring onions and bean sprouts and serve.

EASY		NUTRITIONAL INFORMATION		Serves 4
Preparation Time 20 minutes	**Cooking Time** 20–25 minutes	**Per Serving** 198 calories, 5g fat (of which 1g saturates), 13g carbohydrate, 1.1g salt	Gluten free • Dairy free	

Tandoori Chicken with Cucumber Raita

4 tbsp groundnut oil, plus extra to oil

3 x 150g cartons natural yogurt

juice of ½ lemon

4 skinless chicken breasts, about 600g (1¼lb), cut into finger-width pieces

½ cucumber

salt and ground black pepper

mint leaves to garnish

For the tandoori paste

24 garlic cloves, about 125g (4oz), crushed

5cm (2in) piece fresh root ginger, peeled and chopped

3 tbsp each coriander seeds, cumin seeds, ground fenugreek and paprika

3 red chillies, seeded and chopped (see page 38)

3 tsp English mustard

2 tbsp tomato purée

1 tsp salt

1 Put all the ingredients for the tandoori paste into a food processor with 8 tbsp water and blend to a paste. Divide the paste into three equal portions, freeze two (see Freezing Tips) and put the other in a large bowl.

2 To make the tandoori chicken, add tbsp oil, 2 cartons of yogurt and the lemon juice to the paste. Add the chicken and stir well to coat. Cover the bowl, chill and marinate the chicken for at least 4 hours.

3 Preheat the oven to 220°C (200°C fan oven) mark 7. Oil a roasting tin. Put the chicken in it, drizzle the remaining oil over the chicken and roast for 20 minutes or until cooked through.

4 Meanwhile, prepare the raita. Whisk the remaining carton of yogurt. Using a vegetable peeler, scrape the cucumber into very thin strips. Put the strips in a bowl and pour the whisked yogurt over them. Season, then chill until ready to serve. Garnish the cucumber raita with mint sprigs. Sprinkle the chicken with mint and serve with the raita.

Freezing Tips

At the end of step 1, put two of the portions of tandoori paste into separate freezer bags and freeze. They will keep for up to three months.

To use the frozen paste Put the paste in a microwave and cook on Defrost for 1 minute 20 seconds (based on 900W oven), or thaw at a cool room temperature for 1 hour.

EASY		NUTRITIONAL INFORMATION		Serves
Preparation Time 45 minutes, plus marinating	**Cooking Time** 20 minutes	**Per Serving** 399 calories, 19.9g fat (of which 3.5g saturates), 14.9g carbohydrate, 1.8g salt	Gluten free	**4**

3

Curries

Lamb, Potato and Peanut Curry

2 tbsp olive oil

1 medium onion, chopped

1 tbsp peeled and grated fresh root ginger

1.6kg (3½lb) leg of lamb, diced

3–4 tbsp Massaman paste (see page 12)

1 tbsp fish sauce

2 tbsp peanut butter

100g (3½oz) ground almonds

400ml can coconut milk

600ml (1 pint) hot chicken stock

1–2 tbsp dry sherry

500g (1lb 2oz) small potatoes, peeled and quartered

200g (7oz) green beans, trimmed

75g (3oz) toasted peanuts, roughly chopped

20g pack coriander, finely chopped

2 limes, quartered

rice to serve

1 Preheat the oven to 170°C (150°C fan oven) mark 3. Heat the oil in a large flameproof casserole. Add the onion and cook over a medium heat for 7–8 minutes until golden. Add the ginger and cook for 1 minute. Spoon the onion mixture out of the pan and set aside. Add the lamb and fry in batches until browned. Set aside.

2 Add the Massaman paste, fish sauce and peanut butter to the casserole dish and fry for 2–3 minutes, then add the reserved onion and ginger mixture, lamb pieces, the ground almonds, coconut milk, stock and sherry.

3 Bring to the boil, then cover with a lid and cook in the oven for 1 hour. Add the potatoes and cook for a further 40 minutes, uncovered, adding the green beans for the last 20 minutes. Garnish the curry with toasted peanuts and coriander. Serve with freshly cooked rice and lime wedges to squeeze over the curry.

Serves 8	EASY		NUTRITIONAL INFORMATION	
	Preparation Time 20 minutes	**Cooking Time** about 2 hours	**Per Serving** 664 calories, 47g fat (of which 20.4g saturates), 19g carbohydrate, 0.5g salt	Gluten free • Dairy free

Lamb and Bamboo Shoot Red Curry

2 tbsp sunflower oil

1 large onion, cut into wedges

2 garlic cloves, finely chopped

450g (1lb) lean boneless lamb, cut into 3cm (1¼in) cubes

2 tbsp Thai red curry paste

150ml (¼ pint) lamb or beef stock

2 tbsp Thai fish sauce

2 tsp soft brown sugar

200g can bamboo shoots, drained and thinly sliced

1 red pepper, seeded and thinly sliced

2 tbsp freshly chopped mint

1 tbsp freshly chopped basil

25g (1oz) unsalted peanuts, toasted

rice to serve

1 Heat the oil in a wok or large frying pan, add the onion and garlic and fry over a medium heat for 5 minutes.

2 Add the lamb and curry paste and stir-fry for 5 minutes. Add the stock, fish sauce and sugar. Bring to the boil, then lower the heat, cover and simmer gently for 20 minutes.

3 Stir the bamboo shoots, red pepper and herbs into the curry and cook, uncovered, for a further 10 minutes. Stir in the peanuts and serve immediately, with rice.

EASY		NUTRITIONAL INFORMATION		Serves
Preparation Time 10 minutes	**Cooking Time** 45 minutes	**Per Serving** 397 calories, 25g fat (of which 8g saturates), 17g carbohydrate, 0.4g salt	Gluten free • Dairy free	**4**

Lamb Korma with Red Onion Cachumber

150g carton natural yogurt

700g (1½lb) boneless lamb, cut into 2.5cm (1in) pieces

1 tbsp golden caster sugar

3 tbsp groundnut oil

1 tsp ground turmeric

2 tsp ground coriander

1 small onion, finely chopped

4 garlic cloves, crushed

1cm (½in) piece fresh root ginger, peeled and finely chopped

1 red onion, finely sliced

1 tomato, seeded and diced

1 tbsp chopped mint, plus extra to garnish (optional)

juice of ½ lime

50g (2oz) ground almonds

150ml (¼ pint) double cream

large pinch of saffron

salt and ground black pepper

naan bread to serve

For the korma paste

3 tbsp ground cinnamon

seeds from 36 green cardamom pods

30 cloves

18 bay leaves

1 tbsp fennel seeds

1 tsp salt

1 Put all the ingredients for the korma paste into a food processor and blend to a powder. Tip the powder into a bowl and add 4 tbsp water, stirring well to make a paste. Divide into three equal portions, then freeze two (see page 87) and put the other into a large bowl. To make the curry, add the yogurt, lamb and sugar to the paste in the bowl and mix well. Cover the bowl, chill and leave the lamb to marinate for at least 4 hours, preferably overnight.

2 Preheat the oven to 190°C (170°C fan oven) mark 5. Heat the oil in a flameproof casserole, add the turmeric and coriander and fry for 30 seconds. Add the chopped onion and stir-fry over a high heat for 10 minutes until soft. Add the garlic and ginger and cook for 1–2 minutes. Add the lamb, cover the casserole and cook in the oven for 20 minutes.

3 For the red onion cachumber, put the sliced red onion, tomato, mint and lime juice in a bowl and toss. Season well with salt and chill until needed.

4 Take the casserole out of the oven, and reduce the oven temperature to 170°C (150°C fan oven) mark 3. Add the ground almonds, cream, saffron and 100ml (3½fl oz) water. Season well with salt and pepper and stir together. Cover the casserole, return to the oven and cook for 1½ hours or until the lamb is tender. Serve the lamb korma with naan bread and red onion cachumber, garnished with mint, if you like.

Serves 4	A LITTLE EFFORT		NUTRITIONAL INFORMATION	
	Preparation Time 20 minutes, plus marinating	**Cooking Time** 2 hours	**Per Serving** 714 calories, 56.9g fat (of which 22.2g saturates), 14.9g carbohydrate, 0.5g salt	Gluten free • Dairy free

Curried Lamb with Lentils

500g (1lb 2oz) lean stewing lamb on the bone, cut into 8 pieces (ask your butcher to do this), trimmed of fat

1 tsp ground cumin

1 tsp ground turmeric

2 garlic cloves, crushed

1 medium red chilli, seeded and chopped (see page 38)

2.5cm (1in) piece fresh root ginger, peeled and grated

2 tbsp vegetable oil

1 onion, chopped

400g can chopped tomatoes

2 tbsp vinegar

175g (6oz) red lentils, rinsed

salt and ground black pepper

coriander sprigs to garnish

rocket salad to serve

1 Put the lamb into a shallow, sealable container, add the spices, garlic, chilli, ginger, salt and pepper. Stir well to mix, then cover and chill for at least 30 minutes.

2 Heat the oil in a large flameproof casserole dish, add the onion and cook over a low heat for 5 minutes. Add the lamb and cook for 10 minutes, turning regularly, until the meat is evenly browned.

3 Add the tomatoes, vinegar, 450ml (¾ pint) boiling water and the lentils and bring to the boil. Reduce the heat, cover and simmer for 1 hour. Remove the lid and cook for 30 minutes, stirring occasionally, until the sauce is thick and the lamb is tender. Serve hot, garnished with coriander, with a rocket salad.

EASY		NUTRITIONAL INFORMATION		Serves
Preparation Time 15 minutes, plus marinating	**Cooking Time** 1 hour 50 minutes	**Per Serving** 478 calories, 21.5g fat (of which 7.4g saturates), 36.3g carbohydrate, 0.3g salt	Gluten free • Dairy free	**4**

Thai Beef Curry

4 cloves

1 tsp coriander seeds

1 tsp cumin seeds

seeds from 3 cardamom pods

2 garlic cloves, roughly chopped

2.5cm (1in) piece fresh root ginger, peeled and roughly chopped

1 small onion, roughly chopped

2 tbsp sunflower oil

1 tbsp sesame oil

1 tbsp Thai red curry paste

1 tsp ground turmeric

450g (1lb) sirloin steak, cut into 3cm (1¼in) cubes

225g (8oz) potatoes, peeled and quartered

4 tomatoes, quartered

1 tsp sugar

1 tbsp light soy sauce

300ml (½ pint) coconut milk

150ml (¼ pint) beef stock

4 red chillies, bruised (see Cook's Tip)

50g (2oz) cashew nuts

whole chillies to garnish

rice and stir-fried green vegetables to serve

1 Put the cloves, coriander, cumin and cardamom seeds into a small heavy-based frying pan over a high heat for 1–2 minutes until the spices release their aroma. Leave to cool slightly, then grind to a powder in a spice grinder or blender.

2 Purée the garlic, ginger and onion in a blender or food processor to form a smooth paste. Heat the two oils together in a deep frying pan. Add the onion purée and the curry paste and stir-fry for 5 minutes, then add the roasted ground spices and the turmeric and fry for 5 minutes.

3 Add the beef to the pan and fry for 5 minutes until browned on all sides. Add all the remaining ingredients, except the cashew nuts. Bring to the boil, then reduce the heat, cover the pan and simmer gently for 20–25 minutes until the beef is tender and the potatoes are cooked.

4 Stir in the cashew nuts, garnish with a chilli and serve the curry with plain boiled rice and stir-fried vegetables.

Cook's Tip

Bruise chillies by pressing them under a heavy, flat-bladed knife.

	EASY		NUTRITIONAL INFORMATION	
Serves	**Preparation Time**	**Cooking Time**	**Per Serving**	Gluten free • Dairy free
4	30 minutes	40–45 minutes	484 calories, 27.3g fat (of which 7g saturates), 29.1g carbohydrate, 1.1g salt	

Try Something Different

Instead of chicken, use pork escalopes, cut into thin strips.

Chicken, Bean and Spinach Curry

1 tbsp sunflower oil

350g (12oz) skinless chicken breasts, cut into strips

1 garlic clove, crushed

300–350g tub or jar curry sauce

400g can aduki beans, drained and rinsed

175g (6oz) ready-to-eat dried apricots

150g (5oz) natural bio yogurt, plus extra to serve

125g (4oz) baby spinach leaves

naan bread to serve

1 Heat the oil in a large pan over a medium heat and fry the chicken strips with the garlic until golden. Add the curry sauce, beans and apricots, then cover and simmer gently for 15 minutes or until the chicken is tender.

2 Over a low heat, stir in the yogurt, keeping the curry hot without boiling it, then stir in the spinach until it just begins to wilt. Add a spoonful of yogurt and serve with naan bread.

Serves 4	EASY		NUTRITIONAL INFORMATION	
	Preparation Time 10 minutes	**Cooking Time** about 20 minutes	**Per Serving** 358 calories, 10.6g fat (of which 1.5g saturates), 38g carbohydrate, 2.9g salt	Gluten free

2 tbsp vegetable oil

1 onion, finely sliced

2 garlic cloves, crushed

6 boneless, skinless chicken thighs, cut into strips

2 tbsp tikka masala curry paste

200g can chopped tomatoes

450ml (¾ pint) hot vegetable stock

225g (8oz) baby spinach leaves

fresh coriander leaves to garnish

plain boiled rice, mango chutney and poppadoms to serve

Chicken Tikka Masala

1 Heat the oil in a large pan, add the onion and fry over a medium heat for 5–7 minutes until golden. Add the garlic and chicken and stir-fry for about 5 minutes or until golden.

2 Stir in the curry paste, then add the tomatoes and hot stock. Bring to the boil, then reduce the heat, cover the pan and simmer over a low heat for 15 minutes or until the chicken is cooked through.

3 Add the spinach to the curry, stir and cook until the leaves have just wilted. Garnish with coriander and serve with plain boiled rice, mango chutney and poppadoms.

EASY		NUTRITIONAL INFORMATION		Serves
Preparation Time 15 minutes	**Cooking Time** 30 minutes	**Per Serving** 297 calories, 17g fat (of which 4g saturates), 4g carbohydrate, 0.6g salt	Gluten free • Dairy free	**4**

1 tbsp vegetable oil

3 tbsp Thai red curry paste

4 skinless chicken breasts, about 600g (1lb 5oz), thickly sliced

400ml can coconut milk

300ml (½ pint) hot chicken or vegetable stock

juice of 1 lime

200g pack mixed baby sweetcorn and mangetouts

2 tbsp freshly chopped coriander, plus coriander sprigs to garnish

lime halves and rice or rice noodles to serve

Easy Thai Red Chicken Curry

1 Heat the oil in a wok or large pan over a low heat. Add the curry paste and cook for 2 minutes until fragrant.

2 Add the sliced chicken and fry gently for about 10 minutes until browned.

3 Add the coconut milk, stock, lime juice and baby corn to the pan and bring to the boil. Add the mangetouts, reduce the heat and simmer for 4–5 minutes until the chicken is cooked. Stir in the chopped coriander and serve immediately, garnished with coriander, with rice or noodles and lime halves to squeeze over.

Serves 4	EASY		NUTRITIONAL INFORMATION	
	Preparation Time 5 minutes	**Cooking Time** 20 minutes	**Per Serving** 248 calories, 8g fat (of which 1g saturates), 16g carbohydrate, 1g salt	Gluten free • Dairy free

Thai Green Curry

2 tsp vegetable oil

1 green chilli, seeded and finely chopped (see page 38)

4cm (1½in) piece fresh root ginger, peeled and finely grated

1 lemongrass stalk, cut into 3 pieces

225g (8oz) brown-cap or oyster mushrooms

1 tbsp Thai green curry paste

300ml (½ pint) coconut milk

150ml (¼ pint) chicken stock

1 tbsp Thai fish sauce

1 tsp light soy sauce

350g (12oz) skinless chicken breasts, cut into bite-sized pieces

350g (12oz) cooked and peeled large prawns

fresh coriander sprigs to garnish

rice to serve

1 Heat the oil in a wok or large frying pan, add the chilli, ginger, lemongrass and mushrooms and stir-fry for about 3 minutes or until the mushrooms begin to turn golden. Add the curry paste and fry for a further minute.

2 Pour in the coconut milk, stock, fish sauce and soy sauce and bring to the boil. Stir in the chicken and simmer for about 8 minutes or until the chicken is cooked. Add the prawns and cook for a further minute to heat through. Garnish with coriander sprigs and serve with rice.

EASY		NUTRITIONAL INFORMATION		Serves
Preparation Time 10 minutes	**Cooking Time** 15 minutes	**Per Serving** 132 calories, 2g fat (of which 0g saturates), 4g carbohydrate, 1.4g salt	Dairy free	**6**

Hot Jungle Curry

1 tbsp vegetable oil

350g (12oz) skinless chicken breasts, cut into 5cm (2in) strips

2 tbsp Thai red curry paste

2.5cm (1in) piece fresh root ginger, peeled and thinly sliced

125g (4oz) aubergine, cut into bite-sized pieces

125g (4oz) baby sweetcorn, halved lengthways

75g (3oz) green beans, trimmed

75g (3oz) button or brown-cap mushrooms, halved if large

2–3 kaffir lime leaves (optional)

450ml (¾ pint) chicken stock

2 tbsp Thai fish sauce

grated zest of ½ lime, plus strips of zest to garnish

1 tsp tomato purée

1 tbsp soft brown sugar

steamed rice to serve

1 Heat the oil in a wok or large frying pan. Add the chicken and cook, stirring, for 5 minutes or until the chicken turns golden brown.

2 Add the curry paste and cook for a further minute. Add the ginger, aubergine, sweetcorn, beans, mushrooms and lime leaves, if using, and stir until coated in the curry paste. Add all the remaining ingredients and bring to the boil. Simmer gently for 10–12 minutes or until the chicken and vegetables are just tender. Sprinkle with strips of lime zest and serve with rice.

Try Something Different

Add a drained 225g can of bamboo shoots with the other vegetables in step 2, if you like.

EASY		NUTRITIONAL INFORMATION		Serves
Preparation Time 10 minutes	**Cooking Time** 18–20 minutes	**Per Serving** 160 calories, 5g fat (of which 1g saturates), 5g carbohydrate, 1.1g salt	Gluten free • Dairy free	**4**

Thai Red Turkey Curry

3 tbsp vegetable oil

450g (1lb) onions, finely chopped

200g (7oz) green beans, trimmed

125g (4oz) baby sweetcorn, cut on the diagonal

2 red peppers, seeded and cut into thick strips

1 tbsp Thai red curry paste, or to taste

1 red chilli, seeded and finely chopped (see page 38)

1 lemongrass stalk, very finely chopped

4 kaffir lime leaves, bruised

2 tbsp peeled and finely chopped fresh root ginger

1 garlic clove, crushed

400ml can coconut milk

600ml (1 pint) chicken or turkey stock

450g (1lb) cooked turkey, cut into strips

150g (5oz) bean sprouts

fresh basil leaves to garnish

rice to serve

1 Heat the oil in a wok or large frying pan, add the onions and cook for 4–5 minutes or until soft.

2 Add the beans, sweetcorn and peppers to the pan and stir-fry for 3–4 minutes. Add the curry paste, chilli, lemongrass, lime leaves, ginger and garlic and cook for a further 2 minutes, stirring. Remove from the pan and set aside.

3 Add the coconut milk and stock to the pan, bring to the boil and bubble vigorously for 5–10 minutes until reduced by a quarter.

4 Return the vegetables to the pan with the turkey and bean sprouts. Bring to the boil and simmer for 1–2 minutes until heated through. Garnish with basil leaves and serve with rice.

Serves 6	EASY		NUTRITIONAL INFORMATION	
	Preparation Time 20 minutes	**Cooking Time** about 20 minutes	**Per Serving** 248 calories, 8g fat (of which 1g saturates), 16g carbohydrate, 1.2g salt	Gluten free • Dairy free

Cook's Tip

Buy banana leaves from Asian shops.

Get Ahead

Make the sauce up to 4 hours ahead.
To use Gently reheat to simmering point before you add the fish.

4 skinless sole or plaice fillets, about 125g (4oz) each

2 tbsp light olive oil

1 onion, thinly sliced

1 large garlic clove, crushed

1 green chilli, slit lengthways, seeds left in

2.5cm (1in) piece fresh root ginger, peeled and grated

1 tsp ground turmeric

1 tbsp garam masala (see page 11) or 12 curry leaves (see page 10)

200ml (7fl oz) coconut milk

1 tbsp freshly squeezed lime juice, white wine vinegar or tamarind paste

salt and ground black pepper

fresh banana leaves (optional, see Cook's Tip), basmati rice and 1 lime, cut into wedges, to serve

Kerala Fish Curry

1 Roll up the fish fillets from head to tail, and put to one side.

2 Heat the oil in a deep frying pan over a medium heat and stir in the onion, garlic, chilli and ginger. Stir for 5–7 minutes until the onion is soft. Add the turmeric and garam masala or curry leaves and fry for a further 1–2 minutes until aromatic.

3 Pour the coconut milk into the pan with 200ml (7fl oz) water and bring to the boil. Reduce the heat and simmer very gently, uncovered, for 7–10 minutes until slightly thickened – the consistency of single cream. Stir in the lime juice, vinegar or tamarind. Check the seasoning and adjust if necessary.

4 When ready to serve, carefully lower the fish into the hot sauce and simmer very gently for 1–2 minutes until just cooked. Serve on a bed of basmati rice, in deep bowls lined with strips of banana leaves, if you like, with lime wedges to squeeze over it.

A LITTLE EFFORT		NUTRITIONAL INFORMATION		Serves
Preparation Time 10 minutes	**Cooking Time** about 20 minutes	**Per Serving** 189 calories, 9g fat (of which 1g saturates), 5g carbohydrate, 0.5g salt	Gluten free • Dairy free	**4**

Salmon and Coconut Curry

1 tbsp olive oil

1 red onion, sliced

2 tbsp tikka masala curry paste

4 x 100g (3½oz) salmon steaks

400ml can coconut milk

juice of 1 lime

handful of coriander, roughly chopped

lime wedges to garnish and
boiled rice or naan bread to serve

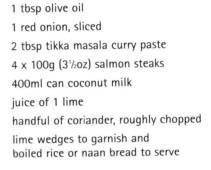

1 Heat the oil in a pan. Add the onion and cook over a medium heat for 10 minutes until soft.

2 Add the curry paste to the pan and cook for 1 minute to warm the spices. Add the fish and cook for 2 minutes, turning it once to coat it in the spices.

3 Pour in the coconut milk and bring to the boil, then reduce the heat and simmer for 5 minutes or until the fish is cooked through. Squeeze the lime juice over it and sprinkle with coriander. Serve with lime wedges to squeeze over the fish and boiled rice or naan bread to soak up the creamy sauce.

Serves 4	EASY		NUTRITIONAL INFORMATION	
	Preparation Time 2 minutes	**Cooking Time** 18 minutes	**Per Serving** 276 calories, 18.6g fat (of which 3.2g saturates), 8.1g carbohydrate, 0.6g salt	Gluten free • Dairy free

Cook's Tip

If you can't find half-fat coconut milk, use half a can of full-fat coconut milk and make up the difference with water or stock. Freeze the remaining milk for up to one month.

Thai Red Seafood Curry

1 tbsp vegetable oil

3 tbsp Thai red curry paste

450g (1lb) monkfish tail, boned to make 350g (12oz) fillet, sliced into rounds

350g (12oz) large raw peeled prawns, deveined

400ml can half-fat coconut milk (see Cook's Tip)

200ml (7fl oz) fish stock

juice of 1 lime

1–2 tbsp Thai fish sauce

125g (4oz) mangetouts

3 tbsp fresh coriander, roughly torn

salt and ground black pepper

1 Heat the oil in a wok or large non-stick frying pan. Add the curry paste and cook for 1–2 minutes.

2 Add the monkfish and prawns and stir well to coat in the curry paste. Add the coconut milk, stock, lime juice and fish sauce. Stir all the ingredients together and bring just to the boil.

3 Add the mangetouts and simmer for 5 minutes or until the mangetouts and fish are tender. Stir in the coriander and check the seasoning, adding salt and pepper to taste. Serve immediately.

EASY		NUTRITIONAL INFORMATION		Serves
Preparation Time 10 minutes	**Cooking Time** 8–10 minutes	**Per Serving** 252 calories, 8g fat (of which 1g saturates), 9g carbohydrate, 2.2g salt	Gluten free • Dairy free	**4**

Prawn Madras with Coconut Chutney

2 tbsp groundnut oil
1 medium onion, finely sliced
1 green chilli, seeded and finely chopped (see page 38)
600ml (1 pint) vegetable stock
450g (1lb) raw king prawns, peeled and deveined
2 bay leaves
coriander leaves to garnish
basmati rice to serve

For the madras paste

1 small onion, finely chopped
2.5cm (1in) piece fresh root ginger, peeled and finely chopped
2 garlic cloves, crushed
juice of ½ lemon
1 tbsp each cumin seeds and coriander seeds
1 tsp cayenne pepper
2 tsp each ground turmeric and garam masala
1 tsp salt

For the coconut chutney

1 tbsp groundnut oil
1 tbsp black mustard seeds
1 medium onion, grated
125g (4oz) desiccated coconut
1 red chilli, seeded and diced (see page 38)

1 Put all the ingredients for the madras paste into a food processor with 2 tbsp water and blend until smooth. Divide the paste into three equal portions, freeze two (see Freezing Tip) and put the other in a large bowel.

2 To make the coconut chutney, heat the oil in a pan and add the mustard seeds. Cover the pan with a lid and cook over a medium heat until the seeds pop – you'll hear them jumping against the lid. Add the grated onion, coconut and red chilli and cook for 3–4 minutes to toast the coconut. Take off the heat and put to one side.

3 To make the curry, heat the oil in a pan, add the onion and fry for 10 minutes until soft and golden. Add the madras paste and green chilli and cook for 5 minutes. Add the stock and bring to the boil. Reduce to a simmer and add the prawns and bay leaves. Cook for 3–5 minutes or until the prawns turn pink. Garnish with coriander and serve with the coconut chutney and basmati rice.

Freezing Tip

At the end of step 1, put two of the portions of madras paste into separate freezer bags and freeze. They will keep for up to three months.
To use the frozen paste Put the paste in a microwave and cook on Defrost for 1 minute 20 seconds (based on a 900W oven), or thaw at a cool room temperature for 1 hour.

A LITTLE EFFORT		NUTRITIONAL INFORMATION		Serves
Preparation Time 10 minutes	**Cooking Time** 25 minutes	**Per Serving** 415 calories, 29.5g fat (of which 17.8g saturates), 14.5g carbohydrate, 1.8g salt	Gluten free • Dairy free	**4**

4

Spicy Suppers

Pork Stir-fry with Chilli and Mango

75g (3oz) medium egg noodles
1 tsp groundnut oil
½ red chilli, seeded and finely chopped (see page 38)
125g (4oz) pork stir-fry strips
1 head pak choi, roughly chopped
1 tbsp soy sauce
½ ripe mango, peeled and sliced

1 Bring a large pan of water to the boil and cook the noodles according to the packet instructions. Drain, then plunge into cold water and put to one side.

2 Meanwhile, heat the oil in a wok or large frying pan until very hot. Add the chilli and pork and stir-fry for 3–4 minutes. Add the pak choi and soy sauce and cook for a further 2–3 minutes. Add the mango and toss to combine.

3 Drain the noodles and add them to the pan. Toss well and cook for 1–2 minutes until heated through. Serve immediately.

Serves	EASY		NUTRITIONAL INFORMATION	
4	**Preparation Time** 5 minutes	**Cooking Time** about 10 minutes	**Per Serving** 138 calories, 3.8g fat (of which 1g saturates), 16.8g carbohydrate, 0.8g salt	Dairy free

Cook's Tip

Instead of the spring-onion butter, brush 16 spring onions lightly with oil and barbecue or grill for 5 minutes. Squeeze some fresh lime juice on top (saves 30 calories per serving) and serve with the corn.

Jamaican-spiced Pork Steaks

2 garlic cloves, crushed

2 small red chillies, finely chopped (including seeds) (see page 38)

1 tsp ground allspice

2 tbsp dark rum

2 tbsp tomato ketchup

4 pork steaks, each weighing about 200g (7oz)

50g (2oz) butter, softened

2 spring onions, thinly sliced

4 corn cobs

salt and ground black pepper

1 Mix together the garlic, chillies, allspice, rum and tomato ketchup. Brush all over the pork steaks, cover and chill for at least 30 minutes or overnight.

2 Mix the butter with the spring onions and plenty of black pepper; put to one side.

3 Preheat the barbecue or grill. Cook the corn cobs in lightly salted boiling water for 2 minutes. Drain well, then barbecue or grill until cooked and beginning to char – about 4–5 minutes. Barbecue or grill the pork for about 5 minutes on each side until cooked through. Serve with the corn, smothered in spring-onion butter.

EASY		NUTRITIONAL INFORMATION		Serves
Preparation Time 20 minutes, plus minimum 30 minutes marinating	**Cooking Time** 10 minutes	**Per Serving** 562 calories, 20.9g fat (of which 10g saturates), 43.8g carbohydrate, 1.7g salt	Gluten free	**4**

Smoky Pimento Goulash

1.1kg (2½lb) braising steak

3 tbsp olive oil

16 shallots or button onions

225g (8oz) piece chorizo sausage, roughly chopped

1 red chilli, seeded and finely chopped (see page 38)

3 bay leaves

3 garlic cloves, crushed

2 tbsp plain flour

2 tbsp smoked paprika

700g jar tomato passata

100ml (3½fl oz) hot beef stock

alt and ground black pepper

mashed potatoes and green vegetables to serve

For the minted soured cream

284ml carton soured cream

1 tbsp finely chopped fresh mint

1 tbsp extra virgin oil, plus extra to drizzle

Get Ahead

Complete the recipe. Cool and chill (it will keep for up to three days) or freeze (it will keep for up to one month).
To use If frozen, thaw overnight at a cool room temperature. Return the goulash to the casserole, bring to the boil and simmer gently for 15–20 minutes until piping hot, adding 100ml (3½fl oz) hot beef stock if it looks dry.

1 Mix together all the ingredients for the minted soured cream and season with a little salt and plenty of coarsely ground black pepper. Cover and chill until needed.

2 Preheat the oven to 170°C (150°C fan oven) mark 3. Cut the braising steak into large cubes, slightly larger than bite-sized.

3 Heat the olive oil in a 4 litre (7 pint) flameproof casserole until really hot. Brown the beef, a few cubes at a time, over a high heat until it is deep brown all over. Remove with a slotted spoon and set aside. Repeat with the remaining beef until all the pieces have been browned.

4 Reduce the heat under the casserole, then add the onions, chorizo, chilli, bay leaves and garlic. Fry for 7–10 minutes until the onions are golden brown and beginning to soften. Return the meat to the casserole and stir in the flour and paprika. Cook, stirring, for 1–2 minutes, then add the passata. Season, cover and cook in the oven for 2½ hours until the beef is meltingly tender. Check halfway through cooking – if the beef looks dry, add 100ml (3½fl oz) hot beef stock. Serve with the minted soured cream, drizzled with a little olive oil and a grinding of black pepper, and some creamy mashed potatoes and green vegetables.

Serves 8	EASY		NUTRITIONAL INFORMATION	
	Preparation Time 20 minutes	**Cooking Time** about 3 hours	**Per Serving** 515 calories, 35.1g fat (of which 13.8g saturates), 13.4g carbohydrate, 1.3g salt	Dairy free

Chilli Bolognese

1 tbsp olive oil

1 large onion, finely chopped

½ large red chilli, seeded and thinly sliced (see page 38)

450g (1lb) minced beef or lamb

125g (4oz) smoked bacon lardons

3 roasted red peppers, drained and finely chopped

400g can chopped tomatoes

125ml (4fl oz) red wine

300g (11oz) spaghetti

25g (1oz) Cheddar or Gruyère cheese, grated plus extra to serve

2 tbsp freshly chopped flat-leafed parsley (optional)

salt and ground black pepper

1 Heat the oil in a large pan over a medium heat. Add the onion and chilli, and fry for 5–10 minutes until soft and golden. Add the beef or lamb and bacon and stir over the heat for 5–7 minutes until well browned.

2 Stir in the red peppers, tomatoes and wine. Season with salt and pepper, bring to the boil, then simmer over a low heat for 15–20 minutes.

3 Meanwhile, cook the spaghetti according to the packet instructions, then drain.

4 Just before serving, stir the grated cheese, parsley, if using, and the sauce into the spaghetti. Sprinkle with cheese and serve.

Serves 4	EASY		NUTRITIONAL INFORMATION
	Preparation Time 15 minutes	**Cooking Time** about 35 minutes	**Per Serving** 761 calories, 33g fat (of which 13g saturates), 74g carbohydrate, 1.4g salt

Chilli Steak and Corn on the Cob

50g (2oz) butter, softened

1 large red chilli, seeded and finely chopped (see page 38)

1 garlic clove, crushed

25g (1oz) Parmesan, freshly grated

1 tbsp finely chopped fresh basil

4 corn cobs, each cut into three

1 tbsp olive oil

4 sirloin steaks, about 150g (5oz) each

mixed green salad to serve

1 Put the butter in a bowl and beat with a wooden spoon. Add the chilli, garlic, Parmesan and basil and mix everything together. Cover and chill to firm up.

2 Bring bring a large pan of water to the boil. Add the corn, cover to bring back to the boil, then simmer, half-covered, for about 10 minutes until tender. Drain well.

3 Heat the oil in a large frying pan or griddle over a medium heat. Cook the steaks for 3–4 minutes on each side for medium-rare (4–5 minutes for medium).

4 Divide the corn and steaks among four warm plates and top with the chilled butter. Serve immediately, with a mixed green salad.

EASY		NUTRITIONAL INFORMATION		Serves
Preparation Time 5 minutes	**Cooking Time** 15 minutes	**Per Serving** 564 calories, 31g fat (of which 14g saturates), 33g carbohydrate, 1.4g salt	Gluten free	**4**

Mexican Chilli Con Carne

2 tbsp olive oil
450g (1lb) minced beef
1 large onion, finely chopped
1 tsp each hot chilli powder and ground cumin
3 tbsp tomato purée
300ml (½ pint) hot vegetable stock
400g can chopped tomatoes with garlic (see Cook's Tips)
25g (1oz) dark chocolate
400g can red kidney beans, drained and rinsed
2 x 20g packs coriander, chopped
salt and ground black pepper
guacamole, salsa, soured cream, grated cheese, tortilla chips and pickled chillies to serve

Cook's Tips

Instead of a can of tomatoes with garlic, use a can of chopped tomatoes and 1 crushed garlic clove.
Adding a little dark chocolate to chilli con carne brings out the flavours of this tasty dish.

1 Heat 1 tbsp oil in a large non-stick pan and fry the beef for 10 minutes until well browned, stirring to break up any lumps. Remove from the pan with a slotted spoon and set aside.

2 Add the remaining oil to the pan, then fry the onion, stirring, for 10 minutes until soft and golden.

3 Add the spices and fry for 1 minute, then return the beef to the pan. Add the tomato purée, stock and tomatoes. Bring to the boil, then reduce to a simmer. Continue to bubble gently, uncovered, for 35–40 minutes, or until the sauce is well reduced and the mixture is quite thick.

4 Stir in the chocolate, kidney beans and coriander, season with salt and pepper, then simmer for 5 minutes.

5 Serve with guacamole, salsa, soured cream, grated cheese, tortilla chips and pickled chillies.

Serves 4	EASY		NUTRITIONAL INFORMATION	
	Preparation Time 5 minutes	**Cooking Time** about 1 hour	**Per Serving** 408 calories, 19.2g fat (of which 6.7g saturates), 28.2g carbohydrate, 1.1g salt	Gluten free • Dairy free

Get Ahead

To prepare ahead, complete the recipe to the end of step 2, cool quickly, cover and chill. It will keep for up to one day. **To use** Bring back to the boil, stir in the pasta and complete the recipe.

Spicy Sausage and Pasta Supper

1 tbsp olive oil

200g (7oz) salami, sliced

225g (8oz) onion, finely chopped

50g (2oz) celery, finely chopped

2 garlic cloves, crushed

400g can pimentos, drained, rinsed and chopped

400g (14oz) passata or 400g can chopped tomatoes

125g (4oz) sun-dried tomatoes in oil, drained

600ml (1 pint) hot chicken or vegetable stock

300ml (½ pint) red wine

1 tbsp sugar

75g (3oz) dried pasta shapes

400g can borlotti beans, drained and rinsed

salt and ground black pepper

freshly chopped flat-leafed parsley to garnish

300ml (½ pint) soured cream and 175g (6oz) Parmesan, freshly grated, to serve

1 Heat the oil in a large pan over a medium heat and fry the salami for 5 minutes or until golden and crisp. Drain on kitchen paper.

2 Fry the onion and celery in the hot oil for 10 minutes or until soft and golden. Add the garlic and fry for 1 minute. Put the salami back in the pan with the pimentos, passata or chopped tomatoes, sun-dried tomatoes, stock, wine and sugar. Bring to the boil.

3 Stir in the pasta, bring back to the boil and cook for about 10 minutes, or according to the packet instructions, until the pasta is almost tender. Stir in the beans and simmer for 3–4 minutes. Top up with more stock if the pasta is not tender when the liquid has been absorbed. Season with salt and pepper.

4 Ladle into warmed bowls and serve topped with soured cream and garnished with the chopped parsley. Serve the grated Parmesan separately.

Serves 6	EASY		NUTRITIONAL INFORMATION	
	Preparation Time 15 minutes	**Cooking Time** 30 minutes	**Per Serving** 564 calories, 35.7g fat (of which 9.7g saturates), 34.4g carbohydrate, 2.6g salt	Dairy free

Grilled Spicy Chicken

4 skinless chicken breasts
1 tbsp coriander seeds, crushed
1 tsp ground cumin
2 tsp mild curry paste
1 garlic clove, crushed
450g (1lb) natural yogurt
3 tbsp freshly chopped coriander
salt and ground black pepper
mixed salad, rice and coriander sprigs to serve

1 Prick the chicken breasts all over with a fork, cover with clingfilm and beat lightly with a rolling pin to flatten them slightly.

2 In a large shallow dish, mix the coriander seeds with the cumin, curry paste, garlic and yogurt. Season with salt and pepper and stir in the chopped coriander. Add the chicken and turn to coat with the spiced yogurt. Cover and leave to marinate in the refrigerator for at least 30 minutes or overnight.

3 Preheat the barbecue or griddle. Lift the chicken out of the marinade and cook over a medium-high heat, turning occasionally, for about 20 minutes or until cooked through. Serve immediately, with rice and a mixed salad, garnished with coriander sprigs.

EASY		NUTRITIONAL INFORMATION		Serves
Preparation Time 10 minutes, plus 30 minutes marinating	**Cooking Time** about 20 minutes	**Per Serving** 266 calories, 7.7g fat (of which 2.3g saturates), 11.1g carbohydrate, 0.5g salt	Gluten free	**4**

Cook's Tip

Scotch bonnets are small but very hot green, yellow or red chillies frequently used in Caribbean cooking.

Caribbean Chicken

10 chicken pieces, such as thighs, drumsticks, wings or breasts, skinned and pierced with a knife

1 tsp salt

1 tbsp ground coriander

2 tsp ground cumin

1 tbsp paprika

pinch of ground nutmeg

1 fresh Scotch bonnet (see Cook's Tip) or other hot red chilli, seeded and chopped (see page 38)

1 onion, chopped

5 fresh thyme sprigs, plus extra to garnish

4 garlic cloves, crushed

2 tbsp dark soy sauce

juice of 1 lemon

2 tbsp vegetable oil

2 tbsp light muscovado sugar

350g (12oz) American easy-cook rice

3 tbsp dark rum (optional)

25g (1oz) butter

2 x 300g cans black-eyed beans, drained and rinsed

ground black pepper

1 Sprinkle the chicken with ½ tsp salt, some pepper, the coriander, cumin, paprika and nutmeg. Add the chilli, onion, thyme and garlic, then pour the soy sauce and lemon juice over the chicken and stir to combine. Cover and chill for at least 4 hours.

2 Heat a 3.4 litre (6 pint) heavy-based pan over a medium heat for 2 minutes. Add the oil and sugar and cook for 3 minutes or until it turns a rich golden caramel colour. (Be careful not to overcook it as it will blacken and taste burnt – watch it very closely.)

3 Remove the chicken pieces from the marinade and add to the caramel mixture in the hot pan. Cover and cook over a medium heat for 5 minutes, then turn the chicken and cook, covered, for another 5 minutes until evenly browned. Add the reserved marinade. Turn the chicken again, then cover and cook for 10 minutes.

4 Add the rice, stir to combine, then pour in 900ml (1½ pints) cold water. Add the rum, if using, the butter and remaining salt. Cover and simmer, without lifting the lid, for 20 minutes or until the rice is tender and most of the liquid has been absorbed.

5 Add the black-eyed beans and mix well. Cover and cook for 3–5 minutes until the beans are warmed through and all the liquid has been absorbed, taking care that the rice doesn't stick to the bottom of the pan. Garnish with fresh thyme and serve hot.

EASY		NUTRITIONAL INFORMATION	Serves
Preparation Time 40 minutes, plus minimum 4 hours marinating	**Cooking Time** 45–50 minutes	**Per Serving** 617 calories, 39g fat (of which 12g saturates), 25g carbohydrate, 2.1g salt	**5**

4 tbsp hot mango chutney (or ordinary mango chutney, plus ½ tsp Tabasco)

grated zest and juice of 1 lime

4 tbsp natural yogurt

2 tbsp freshly chopped coriander, plus extra sprigs to garnish

1 small green chilli (optional), seeded and finely chopped (see page 38)

4 chicken breasts with skin on

1 large ripe mango, peeled and stoned

oil to brush

salt and ground black pepper

lime wedges and rice to serve

Fiery Mango Chicken

1 In a large shallow dish, mix together the chutney, lime zest and juice, yogurt, chopped coriander and, if you would like the dish to be hot and spicy, the chilli.

2 Put the chicken breasts, skin side-down, on the worksurface, cover with clingfilm and beat lightly with a rolling pin. Slice each into three pieces, then put into the yogurt mixture and stir to coat. Cover and chill for at least 30 minutes or overnight.

3 Preheat the barbecue or grill. Slice the mango into four thick pieces. Brush lightly with oil and season well with salt and pepper. Barbecue or grill for about 2 minutes on each side – the fruit should be lightly charred but still firm. Put to one side.

4 Barbecue or grill the chicken for 3–5 minutes on each side until golden. Garnish with coriander and serve with the grilled mango, lime wedges and rice.

Serves 4	EASY		NUTRITIONAL INFORMATION	
	Preparation Time 15 minutes, plus minimum 30 minutes marinating	Cooking Time 10 minutes	Per Serving 297 calories, 14.1g fat (of which 4.1g saturates), 7.8g carbohydrate, 0.3g salt	Gluten free

Chicken with Chorizo and Beans

1 tbsp olive oil
12 chicken pieces (6 drumsticks and 6 thighs)
175g (6oz) chorizo sausage, cubed
1 onion, finely chopped
2 large garlic cloves, crushed
1 tsp mild chilli powder
3 red peppers, seeded and roughly chopped
400g (14oz) passata
2 tbsp tomato purée
300ml (½ pint) chicken stock
2 x 400g cans butter beans, drained and rinsed
200g (7oz) baby new potatoes, halved
1 small bunch of thyme
1 bay leaf
200g (7oz) baby leaf spinach

1 Preheat the oven to 190°C (170°C fan oven) mark 5. Heat the oil in a large flameproof casserole and brown the chicken all over. Remove from the pan and set aside. Add the chorizo to the casserole and fry for 2–3 minutes until its oil starts to run. Add the onion, garlic and chilli powder and fry over a low heat for 5 minutes or until soft.

2 Add the peppers and cook for 2–3 minutes until soft. Stir in the passata, tomato purée, stock, butter beans, potatoes, thyme sprigs and bay leaf. Cover and simmer for 10 minutes.

3 Return the chicken and any juices to the casserole. Bring to a simmer, then cover and cook in the oven for 30–35 minutes. If the sauce looks thin, return the casserole to the hob over a medium heat and simmer to reduce until nicely thick.

4 Remove the thyme and bay leaf, and stir in the spinach until it wilts. Serve immediately.

EASY	NUTRITIONAL INFORMATION		Serves
Preparation Time 10 minutes	**Cooking Time** about 1 hour 10 minutes	**Per Serving** 626 calories, 22g fat (of which 7g saturates), 42g carbohydrate, 3.5g salt	Gluten free • Dairy free	**6**

Cook's Tip

This is a good way to use leftover roast turkey.

Spiced Chicken Pilau

50g (2oz) pinenuts

2 tbsp olive oil

2 onions, sliced

2 garlic cloves, crushed

2 tbsp medium curry powder

6 boneless, skinless chicken thighs or 450g (1lb) skinless cooked chicken, cut into strips

350g (12oz) American easy-cook rice

2 tsp salt

pinch of saffron threads

50g (2oz) sultanas

225g (8oz) ripe tomatoes, roughly chopped

1 Spread the pinenuts over a baking sheet and toast under a hot grill until golden brown, turning them frequently. Put to one side.

2 Heat the oil in a large heavy-based pan over a medium heat. Add the onions and garlic and cook for 5 minutes until soft. Remove half the onion mixture and put to one side.

3 Add the curry powder and cook for 1 minute, then add the chicken and stir. Cook for 10 minutes if the meat is raw, or for 4 minutes if you're using cooked chicken, stirring from time to time until browned.

4 Add the rice, stir to coat in the oil, then add 900ml (1½ pints) boiling water, the salt and saffron. Cover and bring to the boil. Reduce the heat to low and cook for 20 minutes or until the rice is tender and most of the liquid has been absorbed. Stir in the reserved onion mixture, the sultanas, tomatoes and pinenuts. Cook for 5 minutes to warm through, then serve.

Serves 4	EASY		NUTRITIONAL INFORMATION	
	Preparation Time 15 minutes	Cooking Time 35–40 minutes	Per Serving 649 calories, 18g fat (of which 2g saturates), 87g carbohydrate, 2.8g salt	Gluten free • Dairy free

Try Something Different

Replace the chicken with pork escalopes or rump steak, cut into thin strips.

4 skinless chicken breasts, cut into strips

1 tbsp ground coriander

2 garlic cloves, finely chopped

4 tbsp vegetable oil

2 tbsp clear honey

fresh coriander sprigs to garnish

Thai fragrant rice to serve

For the peanut sauce

1 tbsp vegetable oil

2 tbsp curry paste

2 tbsp brown sugar

2 tbsp peanut butter

200ml (7fl oz) coconut milk

Chicken with Peanut Sauce

1 Mix the chicken with the ground coriander, garlic, oil and honey. Cover, chill and leave to marinate for 15 minutes.

2 To make the peanut sauce, heat the oil in a pan, add the curry paste, sugar and peanut butter and fry for 1 minute. Add the coconut milk and bring to the boil, stirring all the time, then simmer for 5 minutes.

3 Meanwhile, heat a wok or large frying pan and, when hot, stir-fry the chicken and its marinade in batches for 3–4 minutes or until cooked, adding more oil if needed.

4 Serve the chicken on a bed of Thai fragrant rice, with the peanut sauce poured over it. Garnish with coriander sprigs.

EASY		NUTRITIONAL INFORMATION		Serves
Preparation Time 10 minutes, plus 15 minutes marinating	**Cooking Time** about 10 minutes	**Per Serving** 408 calories, 20g fat (of which 3g saturates), 19g carbohydrate, 0.5g salt	Gluten free • Dairy free	**4**

Cook's Tip

Quinoa is a grain, first grown by the Incas, that can be used in place of rice. It has a mild flavour and slightly chewy texture.

2 tbsp mango chutney

juice of ½ lemon

1 tbsp olive oil

2 tsp mild curry powder

1 tsp paprika

350g (12oz) skinless chicken breast, cut into thick strips

200g (7oz) quinoa (see Cook's Tip)

1 cucumber, roughly chopped

½ bunch of spring onions, sliced

50g (2oz) ready-to-eat dried apricots, sliced

2 tbsp freshly chopped mint, basil or tarragon

salt and ground black pepper

mint leaves to garnish

Mild Spiced Chicken with Quinoa

1 Put the chutney, lemon juice, ½ tbsp oil, the curry powder and paprika into a bowl and mix together. Add the chicken and toss to coat.

2 Cook the quinoa in boiling water for 10–12 minutes until tender, or according to the packet instructions. Drain thoroughly. Put into a bowl, then stir in the cucumber, spring onions, apricots, herbs and remaining oil. Season with salt and pepper.

3 Meanwhile, put the chicken and marinade into a pan and fry over a high heat for 2–3 minutes, then add 150ml (¼ pint) water. Bring to the boil, then simmer for 5 minutes or until the chicken is cooked. Serve with the quinoa and garnish with mint leaves.

Serves 4	EASY		NUTRITIONAL INFORMATION	
	Preparation Time 15 minutes	**Cooking Time** 10–12 minutes	**Per Serving** 268 calories, 3g fat (of which trace saturates), 37g carbohydrate, 0.4g salt	Gluten free • Dairy free

Lime and Chilli Swordfish

1 tsp dried chilli flakes

4 tbsp olive oil

grated zest and juice of 1 lime, plus 1 whole lime, sliced, to serve

1 garlic clove, crushed

4 x 175g (6oz) swordfish steaks

salt and ground black pepper

mixed salad to serve

1 Put the chilli flakes in a large shallow bowl. Add the oil, lime zest and juice and garlic and mix everything together. Add the swordfish steaks to the marinade and toss several times to coat completely. Leave to marinate for 30 minutes.

2 Preheat the barbecue or preheat a griddle pan until hot.

3 Lift the swordfish out of the marinade, season well with salt and pepper, and then cook the steaks for 2 minutes on each side. Top with slices of lime and continue to cook for 1 minute or until the fish is opaque right through. Serve immediately, with a mixed salad.

EASY		NUTRITIONAL INFORMATION		Serves
Preparation Time 10 minutes, plus 30 minutes marinating	**Cooking Time** 5 minutes	**Per Serving** 216 calories, 10g fat (of which 2g saturates), 0g carbohydrate, 0.6g salt	Gluten free • Dairy free	**4**

Cook's Tips

Furikake seasoning is a Japanese condiment consisting of sesame seeds and chopped seaweed. It can be found in major supermarkets and Asian food shops.

Soba noodles are made from buckwheat and are gluten free. If you have a wheat allergy or gluten intolerance, check that the pack specifies '100% soba'.

Teriyaki Salmon with Spinach

550g (1¼lb) salmon fillet, cut into 1cm (½in) slices
3 tbsp teriyaki sauce
3 tbsp tamari or light soy sauce
2 tbsp vegetable oil
1 tbsp sesame oil
1 tbsp chopped fresh chives
2 tsp peeled and grated fresh root ginger
2 garlic cloves, crushed
350g (12oz) soba noodles (see Cook's Tips)
350g (12oz) baby spinach leaves
furikake seasoning (see Cook's Tips)

1 Gently mix the salmon slices with the teriyaki sauce, then cover, chill and leave to marinate for 1 hour.

2 Mix together the tamari or soy sauce, 1 tbsp vegetable oil, the sesame oil, chives, ginger and garlic. Set aside.

3 Cook the noodles according to the packet instructions. Drain and put to one side.

4 Heat the remaining vegetable oil in a wok or large frying pan. Remove the salmon from the marinade and add it to the pan. Cook over a high heat until it turns opaque – about 30 seconds. Remove from the pan and put to one side. Add the drained noodles to the pan and stir until warmed through. Stir in the spinach and cook for 1–2 minutes until wilted. Add the soy sauce mixture and stir to combine.

5 Divide the noodles among four bowls, top with the salmon. Sprinkle with furikake seasoning and serve.

Serves	EASY		NUTRITIONAL INFORMATION	
4	**Preparation Time** 10 minutes, plus 1 hour marinating	**Cooking Time** 6 minutes	**Per Serving** 672 calories, 30g fat (of which 4g saturates), 66g carbohydrate, 2.9g salt	Gluten free • Dairy free

Try Something Different

There are plenty of alternatives to cod: try coley (saithe), sea bass or pollack.

2 tsp olive oil

1 shallot, chopped

1 tbsp Thai green curry paste

225g (8oz) brown basmati rice

600ml (1 pint) hot fish or vegetable stock

150ml (¼ pint) half-fat coconut milk

350g (12oz) skinless cod fillet, cut into bite-sized pieces

350g (12oz) sugarsnap peas

125g (4oz) cooked and peeled prawns

25g (1oz) flaked almonds, toasted

squeeze of lemon juice

salt and ground black pepper

2 tbsp freshly chopped coriander to garnish

Coconut Fish Pilau

1 Heat the oil in a frying pan, add the shallot and 1 tbsp water and fry for 4–5 minutes until golden. Stir in the curry paste and cook for 1–2 minutes.

2 Add the rice, stock and coconut milk. Bring to the boil, then cover and simmer for 15–20 minutes until all the liquid has been absorbed.

3 Add the cod and cook for 3–5 minutes. Add the sugarsnap peas, prawns, almonds and lemon juice and stir over the heat for 3–4 minutes until heated through. Check the seasoning and serve immediately, garnished with coriander.

EASY		NUTRITIONAL INFORMATION		Serves
Preparation Time 15 minutes	**Cooking Time** 30 minutes	**Per Serving** 398 calories, 7g fat (of which 1g saturates), 53g carbohydrate, 0.4g salt	Gluten free • Dairy free	**4**

Cook's Tip

Gumbo is a traditional stew from the southern states of the USA, containing meat, vegetables and shellfish and thickened with okra.

Seafood Gumbo

125g (4oz) butter

50g (2oz) plain flour

1–2 tbsp Cajun spice

1 onion, chopped

1 green pepper, seeded and chopped

5 spring onions, sliced

1 tbsp freshly chopped flat-leafed parsley

1 garlic clove, crushed

1 beef tomato, chopped

125g (4oz) garlic sausage, finely sliced

75g (3oz) American easy-cook rice

1.2 litres (2 pints) vegetable stock

250g (9oz) okra, sliced

1 bay leaf

1 fresh thyme sprig

2 tsp salt

¼ tsp cayenne pepper

juice of ½ lemon

4 cloves

175g (6oz) raw tiger prawns

175g (6oz) raw mussels in their shells, scrubbed and debearded

150g (5oz) squid tubes, sliced

ground black pepper

crusty bread to serve

1 Heat the butter in a 2.5 litre (4¼–4½ pint) heavy-based pan over a low heat. Add the flour and Cajun spice and cook, stirring, for 1–2 minutes until golden brown. Add the onion, green pepper, spring onions, parsley and garlic and cook for 5 minutes.

2 Add the tomato, garlic sausage and rice to the pan and stir well to coat. Add the stock, okra, bay leaf, thyme, salt, cayenne pepper, lemon juice and cloves. Season with black pepper. Bring to the boil and simmer, covered, for 12 minutes or until the rice is tender.

3 Add the seafood and cook for 3–4 minutes, until the prawns are pink and the mussels have opened. Discard any mussels that are still closed. Serve the gumbo in deep bowls with bread.

EASY		NUTRITIONAL INFORMATION	Serves
Preparation Time 10 minutes	**Cooking Time** 30 minutes	**Per Serving** 607 calories, 38.1g fat (of which 21.2g saturates), 41.8g carbohydrate, 1.6g salt	**4**

Curried Coconut and Vegetable Rice

1 large aubergine, about 300g (11oz), trimmed

1 large butternut squash, about 500g (1lb 2oz), peeled and seeded

250g (9oz) dwarf green beans, trimmed

100ml (3½fl oz) vegetable oil

1 large onion, chopped

1 tbsp black mustard seeds

3 tbsp korma paste (see page 12)

350g (12oz) basmati rice

400ml can coconut milk

200g (7oz) baby spinach leaves

salt and ground black pepper

1 Cut the aubergine and butternut squash into 2cm (¾in) cubes. Slice the green beans into 2cm (¾in) pieces.

2 Heat the oil in a large pan. Add the onion and cook for about 5 minutes until a light golden colour. Add the mustard seeds and cook, stirring, until they begin to pop. Stir in the korma paste and cook for 1 minute.

3 Add the aubergine and cook, stirring, for 5 minutes. Add the butternut squash, beans, rice and 2 tsp salt, mixing well. Pour in the coconut milk and add 600ml (1 pint) water. Bring to the boil, cover and simmer for 15–18 minutes.

4 When the rice and vegetables are cooked, remove the lid and put the spinach leaves on top. Cover and leave, off the heat, for 5 minutes. Gently stir the wilted spinach through the rice, check the seasoning and serve immediately.

Serves 6	EASY		NUTRITIONAL INFORMATION	
	Preparation Time 15 minutes	**Cooking Time** 30 minutes, plus 5 minutes standing	**Per Serving** 413 calories, 16.8g fat (of which 1.9g saturates), 57.1g carbohydrate, 0.4g salt	Vegetarian Gluten free • Dairy free

5

Vegetarian Dishes

Moroccan Chickpea Stew

Spicy Vegetable Kebabs

Black-eyed Bean Chilli

Spiced Egg Pilau

Mauritian Vegetable Curry

Tofu Laksa Curry

Aubergine and Pepper Balti with Carrot Relish

Lentil Chilli

Chickpea and Chilli Stir-fry

Chilli Vegetable and Coconut Stir-fry

Moroccan Chickpea Stew

1 red pepper, halved and seeded

1 green pepper, halved and seeded

1 yellow pepper, halved and seeded

2 tbsp olive oil

1 onion, finely sliced

2 garlic cloves, crushed

1 tbsp harissa paste

2 tbsp tomato purée

½ tsp ground cumin

1 aubergine, diced

400g can chickpeas, drained and rinsed

450ml (¾ pint) vegetable stock

4 tbsp roughly chopped flat-leafed parsley, plus a few sprigs to garnish

salt and ground black pepper

crusty bread to serve

1 Preheat the grill and lay the peppers, skin-side up, on a baking sheet. Grill for around 5 minutes until the skin begins to blister and char. Put the peppers in a plastic bag, seal and put to one side for a few minutes. When cooled a little, peel off the skins and discard, then slice the peppers and put to one side.

2 Heat the oil in a large heavy-based frying pan over a low heat, add the onion and cook for 5–10 minutes until soft. Add the garlic, harissa, tomato purée and cumin and cook for 2 minutes.

3 Add the peppers to the pan with the aubergine. Stir everything to coat evenly with the spices and cook for 2 minutes. Add the chickpeas and stock, season well with salt and pepper and bring to the boil. Simmer for 20 minutes.

4 Just before serving, stir the chopped parsley through the chickpea stew. Garnish with parsley sprigs and serve with crusty bread.

Serves 4	EASY		NUTRITIONAL INFORMATION	
	Preparation Time 10 minutes	**Cooking Time** 40 minutes	**Per Serving** 232 calories, 9g fat (of which 1g saturates), 29g carbohydrate, 0.6g salt	Vegetarian Gluten free • Dairy free

Cook's Tip

Yogurt Sauce: mix together 225g (8oz) Greek yogurt, 1 crushed garlic clove and 2 tbsp freshly chopped coriander. Season with salt and pepper. Chill until ready to serve.

12 baby onions

12 new potatoes

12 button mushrooms

2 courgettes

2 garlic cloves, crushed

1 tsp each ground coriander and turmeric

½ tsp ground cumin

1 tbsp sun-dried tomato paste

1 tsp chilli sauce

juice of ½ lemon

4 tbsp olive oil

275g (10oz) smoked tofu, cut into 2.5cm (1in) cubes

salt and ground black pepper

Yogurt Sauce (see Cook's Tip) and lemon wedges to serve

Spicy Vegetable Kebabs

1 Blanch the baby onions in a pan of boiling salted water for 3 minutes; drain, refresh in cold water and peel away the skins. Put the potatoes into a pan of cold salted water, bring to the boil and parboil for 8 minutes; drain and refresh under cold water. Blanch the button mushrooms in boiling water for 1 minute; drain and refresh under cold water. Cut each courgette into six chunky slices and blanch for 1 minute; drain and refresh.

2 Mix the garlic, spices, tomato paste, chilli sauce, lemon juice, olive oil, salt and pepper together in a shallow dish. Add the well-drained vegetables and tofu and toss to coat. Cover and chill for several hours or overnight.

3 Preheat the barbecue or grill. Soak six wooden skewers in water for 20 minutes. Thread the vegetables and tofu on to the skewers. Cook the kebabs for 8–10 minutes until the vegetables are charred and tender, turning frequently and basting with the marinade. Serve with Yogurt Sauce and lemon wedges.

EASY		NUTRITIONAL INFORMATION		Serves
Preparation Time 30 minutes, plus marinating	**Cooking Time** 25 minutes	**Per Serving** 247 calories, 14g fat (of which 3g saturates), 22g carbohydrate, 0.1g salt	Vegetarian Gluten free	**4**

Black-Eyed Bean Chilli

1 tbsp olive oil

1 onion, chopped

3 celery sticks, finely chopped

2 x 400g cans black-eyed beans, drained and rinsed

2 x 400g cans chopped tomatoes

2 or 3 splashes of Tabasco sauce

3 tbsp freshly chopped coriander

4 warmed tortillas and soured cream to serve

1 Heat the oil in a frying pan. Add the onion and celery and cook for 10 minutes until softened.

2 Add the beans, tomatoes and Tabasco to the pan. Bring to the boil, then simmer for 10 minutes.

3 Just before serving, stir in the coriander. Spoon the chilli on to the warm tortillas, roll up and serve with soured cream.

Serves	EASY		NUTRITIONAL INFORMATION	
4	**Preparation Time** 10 minutes	**Cooking Time** 20 minutes	**Per Serving** 245 calories, 5g fat (of which 1g saturates), 39g carbohydrate, 1.8g salt	Vegetarian

Cook's Tip

Coconut cream is sold in cartons, has a thick creamy texture and can be used in sweet and savoury dishes.
Creamed coconut is a solid block of coconut, which can be grated or crumbled into sauces to thicken them. It can also be dissolved in hot water to make coconut cream for this recipe: roughly chop 125g (4oz) coconut cream, add 200ml (7fl oz) hot water, leave for 5 minutes, then beat well until smooth.

Spiced Egg Pilau

200g (7oz) basmati or wild rice
150g (5oz) frozen peas
4 medium eggs
200ml (7fl oz) coconut cream (see Cook's Tip)
1 tsp mild curry paste
1 tbsp sweet chilli sauce
1 tbsp smooth peanut butter
1 large bunch of coriander, roughly chopped
mini poppadoms and mango chutney to serve

1 Put the rice in a pan with 450ml (¾ pint) boiling water, set over a low heat and cook for 15 minutes or until just tender. Add the peas for the last 5 minutes of cooking time.

2 Meanwhile, put the eggs into a large pan of boiling water and simmer for 6 minutes, then drain and shell.

3 Put the coconut cream, curry paste, chilli sauce and peanut butter into a small pan and whisk together. Heat the sauce gently, stirring, without allowing it to boil.

4 Drain the rice and stir in the chopped coriander and 2 tbsp of the sauce.

5 Divide the rice among four bowls. Cut the eggs into halves and serve on the rice, spooning the remaining coconut sauce over the top. Serve with poppadums and mango chutney.

EASY		NUTRITIONAL INFORMATION		Serves
Preparation Time 5 minutes	**Cooking Time** 15 minutes	**Per Serving** 331 calories, 9g fat (of which 12g saturates), 50g carbohydrate, 0.6g salt	Vegetarian Gluten free • Dairy free	**4**

Get Ahead

To prepare ahead, complete the recipe, without the garnish, and chill quickly. It will keep in the refrigerator for up to two days.
To use Put in a pan, cover and bring to the boil, then simmer for 10–15 minutes. Garnish and serve.

Mauritian Vegetable Curry

3 tbsp vegetable oil

1 onion, finely sliced

4 garlic cloves, crushed

2.5cm (1in) piece fresh root ginger, peeled and grated

3 tbsp medium curry powder

6 fresh curry leaves

150g (5oz) potato, peeled and cut into 1cm (½in) cubes

125g (4oz) aubergine, cut into 2cm (1in) sticks, 5mm (¼in) wide

150g (5oz) carrots, peeled and cut into 5mm (¼in) dice

900ml (1½ pints) vegetable stock

pinch of saffron threads

1 tsp salt

150g (5oz) green beans, trimmed

75g (3oz) frozen peas

ground black pepper

3 tbsp chopped fresh coriander to garnish

1 Heat the oil in a large heavy-based pan over a low heat. Add the onion and fry for 5–10 minutes until golden. Add the garlic, ginger, curry powder and curry leaves and fry for a further minute.

2 Add the potato and aubergine to the pan and fry, stirring, for 2 minutes. Add the carrots, stock, saffron and salt. Season with plenty of pepper. Cover and cook for 10 minutes until the potato and carrots are almost tender.

3 Add the beans and peas to the pan and cook for a further 4 minutes. Sprinkle with the chopped coriander and serve.

Serves 4	EASY		NUTRITIONAL INFORMATION	
	Preparation Time 15 minutes	**Cooking Time** 25–30 minutes	**Per Serving** 184 calories, 11g fat (of which 1g saturates), 18g carbohydrate, 1.7g salt	Vegetarian Gluten free • Dairy free

2 tbsp light soy sauce

½ red chilli, seeded and chopped (see page 38)

5cm (2in) piece fresh root ginger, peeled and grated

250g pack fresh tofu

1 tbsp olive oil

1 onion, finely sliced

3 tbsp laksa paste

200ml (7fl oz) coconut milk

900ml (1½ pints) hot vegetable stock

200g (7oz) baby sweetcorn, halved lengthways

200g (7oz) fine green beans, trimmed

250g pack medium rice noodles

salt and ground black pepper

2 spring onions, sliced diagonally, 2 tbsp chopped coriander and 1 lime, cut into four wedges, to garnish

Tofu Laksa Curry

1 Put the soy sauce, chilli and ginger in a bowl, add the tofu and leave to marinate.

2 Heat the oil in a large pan. Add the onion and fry over a medium heat for 10 minutes, stirring, until golden. Add the laksa paste and cook for 2 minutes. Add the tofu, coconut milk, hot stock and sweetcorn and season. Bring to the boil, add the green beans, reduce the heat and simmer for 8–10 minutes.

3 Meanwhile, put the noodles in a large bowl, pour boiling water over them and soak for 30 seconds. Drain, then stir into the curry. Pour into bowls and garnish with the spring onions, coriander and lime wedges. Serve immediately.

EASY		NUTRITIONAL INFORMATION		Serves
Preparation Time 15 minutes	**Cooking Time** 22 minutes	**Per Serving** 349 calories, 7.1g fat (of which 0.9g saturates), 59g carbohydrate, 1.4g salt	Vegetarian Dairy free	**4**

Aubergine and Pepper Balti with Carrot Relish

4 tbsp groundnut oil, plus 1 tsp for the relish

1 onion, finely sliced

1 aubergine, cut into 2cm (¾in) dice

1 red and 1 green chilli, seeded and roughly chopped (see page 38)

1 red and 1 green pepper, seeded and sliced

4 tomatoes, about 300g (11oz), quartered

600ml (1 pint) vegetable stock

2 tsp black mustard seeds

450g (1lb) carrots, peeled and grated

2 tbsp tamarind paste

2 tbsp dark muscovado sugar

1 tbsp white wine vinegar

50g (2oz) baby spinach leaves

salt and ground black pepper

pilau rice to serve

For the balti paste

1 tbsp each fennel seeds and ground allspice

2–3 garlic cloves, roughly chopped

1cm (½in) piece fresh root ginger, peeled and roughly chopped

50g (2oz) garam masala (see page 11)

25g (1oz) curry powder (see page 11)

1 tsp salt

1 Put all the ingredients for the balti paste into a food processor with 8 tbsp water and blend. Divide the paste into three equal portions, freeze two (see page 87) and put the other to one side.

2 To make the curry, heat 4 tbsp oil in a large flameproof casserole and fry the onion over a high heat for 10–15 minutes until golden. Add the aubergine and cook for another 5 minutes.

3 Add the balti paste and the chillies to the casserole, stir well to mix and cook for 1–2 minutes. Add the peppers and tomatoes and cook for 5 minutes, then add the stock and season well. Cover and bring to the boil, then reduce the heat and simmer the balti for 15 minutes or until the vegetables are tender.

4 Meanwhile, make the carrot relish. Heat the 1 tsp oil in a pan and add the mustard seeds. Cover with a lid and cook until they start to pop – you'll hear them jumping against the lid. Add the carrots, tamarind paste, sugar and vinegar to the pan and cook for 1–2 minutes. Stir well.

5 Stir the spinach into the curry and serve with the carrot relish and pilau rice to soak up the sauce.

Serves 4	EASY		NUTRITIONAL INFORMATION	
	Preparation Time 30 minutes	**Cooking Time** 45 minutes	**Per Serving** 364 calories, 17.6g fat (of which 2g saturates), 46.5g carbohydrate, 0.4g salt	Vegetarian Gluten free • Dairy free

Cook's Tip

Oil-water spray is far lower in calories than oil alone and, as it sprays on thinly and evenly, you'll use less. Fill one-eighth of a travel-sized spray bottle with oil such as sunflower, light olive or vegetable (rapeseed) oil, then top up with water. To use, shake well before spraying. Store in the refridgerator.

Lentil Chilli

oil-water spray (see Cook's Tip)

2 red onions, chopped

1½ tsp each ground coriander and ground cumin

½ tsp ground paprika

2 garlic cloves, crushed

2 sun-dried tomatoes, chopped

¼ tsp crushed dried chilli flakes

125ml (4fl oz) red wine

300ml (½ pint) vegetable stock

2 x 400g cans brown or green lentils, drained and rinsed

2 x 400g cans chopped tomatoes

sugar to taste

salt and ground black pepper

natural low-fat yogurt and rice to serve

1 Spray a large pan with the oil-water spray and add the onions and cook for 5 minutes until softened. Add the coriander, cumin and paprika. Combine the garlic, sun-dried tomatoes, chilli flakes, wine and stock and add to the pan. Cover and simmer for 5–7 minutes. Uncover and simmer until the onions are very tender and the liquid has almost gone.

2 Stir in the lentils and tomatoes and season with salt and pepper. Simmer, uncovered, for 15 minutes until thick. Stir in sugar to taste. Remove from the heat.

3 Ladle out a quarter of the mixture and blend in a food processor or blender. Combine the puréed and unpuréed portions. Serve with yogurt and rice.

Serves	EASY		NUTRITIONAL INFORMATION	
6	**Preparation Time** 10 minutes	**Cooking Time** 30 minutes	**Per Serving** 191 calories, 2g fat (of which trace saturates), 30g carbohydrate, 0g salt	Vegetarian Gluten free • Dairy free

Chickpea and Chilli Stir-fry

2 tbsp olive oil

1 tsp ground cumin

1 red onion, sliced

2 garlic cloves, finely chopped

1 red chilli, seeded and finely chopped (see page 38)

2 x 400g cans chickpeas, drained and rinsed

400g (14oz) cherry tomatoes

125g (4oz) baby spinach leaves

salt and ground black pepper

brown rice or pasta to serve

1 Heat the oil in a wok or large frying pan. Add the cumin and fry for 1–2 minutes. Add the onion and stir-fry for 5–7 minutes.

2 Add the garlic and chilli and stir-fry for 2 minutes.

3 Add the chickpeas to the wok with the tomatoes. Reduce the heat and simmer until the chickpeas are hot. Season with salt and pepper, then add the spinach and stir until just wilted. Serve with brown rice or pasta.

EASY		NUTRITIONAL INFORMATION		Serves
Preparation Time 10 minutes	**Cooking Time** 15–20 minutes	**Per Serving** 258 calories, 11g fat (of which 1g saturates), 30g carbohydrate, 1g salt	Vegetarian Gluten free • Dairy free	**4**

Chilli Vegetable and Coconut Stir-fry

125g (4oz) each carrots, baby sweetcorn and mangetouts

2.5cm (1in) piece fresh root ginger, peeled

2 tbsp sesame oil

2 green chillies, seeded and finely chopped (see page 38)

2 garlic cloves, crushed

1 tbsp Thai green curry paste

2 large red peppers, finely sliced

2 small pak choi, quartered

4 spring onions, finely chopped

300ml (½ pint) coconut milk

2 tbsp peanut satay sauce

2 tbsp light soy sauce

1 tsp soft brown sugar

4 tbsp freshly chopped coriander, plus extra sprigs to garnish

ground black pepper

roasted peanuts to garnish

rice or noodles to serve

1 Peel the carrots and cut into fine matchsticks. Cut the sweetcorn in half lengthways. Halve the mangetouts on the diagonal. Finely grate the ginger.

2 Heat the oil in a wok or large non-stick frying pan over a medium heat and stir-fry the chillies, ginger and garlic for 1 minute. Add the curry paste and fry for a further 30 seconds.

3 Add the carrots, sweetcorn, mangetouts and red peppers. Stir-fry over a high heat for 3–4 minutes, then add the pak choi and spring onions. Cook, stirring, for a further 1–2 minutes.

4 Pour in the coconut milk, satay sauce, soy sauce and sugar. Season with pepper, bring to the boil and cook for 1–2 minutes, then add the chopped coriander. Garnish with the peanuts and coriander sprigs and serve with rice or noodles.

Serves 4	EASY		NUTRITIONAL INFORMATION	
	Preparation Time 25 minutes	**Cooking Time** about 10 minutes	**Per Serving** 200 calories, 11.1g fat (of which 2.1g saturates), 20.6g carbohydrate, 1.4g salt	Vegetarian • Dairy free

Index